"The key to boosting your self-esteem is to change not just how you think, but what you do. That's the light bulb idea in Hartwell-Walker's eye-opening, empowering new book."

—**Marianne Wait**, health editor and writer

"This book is a winner! After convincing us that *genuine* self-esteem must combine *doing good* in the world with *thinking good* about yourself, it shows in clear, practical ways how to progress toward those goals. Hartwell-Walker's step-by-step approach for improving genuine self-esteem begins with a chapter on building one's initial commitment. This is followed by chapters on improved 'self-care,' courage, positivity, and building rewarding relationships. The book is remarkable in that it advances the reader through a series of self-assessments that build upon one another. Hartwell-Walker is not only an experienced therapist and advice columnist, but also a skilled writer whose language is clear and accessible. She connects her readers with inspiring examples that make excellent reading."

—**George Levinger**, emeritus professor of psychology at the University of Massachusetts Amherst

UNLOCKING
the SECRETS of
SELF-ESTEEM

A GUIDE to BUILDING CONFIDENCE and CONNECTION ONE STEP at a TIME

MARIE HARTWELL-WALKER, EdD

NEW HARBINGER PUBLICATIONS, INC.

Publisher's Note

Distributed in Canada by Raincoast Books

Copyright © 2015 by Marie Hartwell-Walker
        New Harbinger Publications, Inc.
        5674 Shattuck Avenue
        Oakland, CA 94609
        www.newharbinger.com

Cover design by Amy Shoup
Acquired by Jess O'Brien
Edited by Jasmine Star

Library of Congress Cataloging-in-Publication Data on file

Printed in the United States of America

17   16   15

10 9 8 7 6 5 4 3 2 1   First printing

For my family

Contents

Foreword

Over my twenty-year career, one of the questions I've been asked most frequently is, *How can I get more self-esteem?* People have a general understanding that *more* self-esteem is good and that *poor* self-esteem leads to all sorts of additional problems in a person's life.

It's never been an easy question to answer. I've always had a difficult time explaining how exactly one goes about obtaining "good" self-esteem, and I certainly couldn't lay out a set of easy steps one could take to get there. It's not as if there's a self-esteem store one can just visit and make a purchase.

The problem for me was twofold. First, like many people, I underestimated what self-esteem is truly all about. I didn't fully grasp how complex this simple idea actually is. Second, I didn't understand how I came to have good self-esteem in the first place.

The foundation of my self-esteem was laid for me in early childhood through a combination of a hearty work ethic and the view that one could always improve one's circumstances in life. My parents served as good role models, having uprooted their lives to move from a backwoods Pennsylvania coal town to a developing, suburban college town that granted us more opportunities.

When they made the decision to move far away from all of their family and friends, they didn't know if they'd make it in the end. The move took courage and optimism on their part. They just believed that they could, if they only worked hard and did good work in raising their family.

And that's the difference between what most people think of as self-esteem and what this book is all about: *genuine* self-esteem.

Genuine self-esteem comes not only from feeling good about yourself but also from what you actually do. Actions help define us—more than most people realize. We all have to make difficult decisions in life with no guarantee of a positive outcome. But people with genuine self-esteem try to make decisions that are ethical, moral, and ultimately good. Such everyday decisions and behaviors shape the very way we think about others—and ourselves.

These insights come not from me but rather from Marie Hartwell-Walker, whom I've known most of my professional career. She's been an amazing contributor to Psych Central over the years in many different capacities. What I've often been struck by is her thoughtful analysis of a problem. Far more than anyone else I've known, she can break something down into meaningful pieces and then put them back together in a way that is newly helpful.

We are awash in self-help books and apps that promise to help us change practically anything about our lives: make us happier, help us break bad habits, motivate us to do the things we don't want to do. Too many of these books are based upon one person's experiences and illustrative anecdotes. Too many apps are created by developers who majored in psychology in college and believe that provides them all they need to know about the complexities of human behavior and behavior change. Too few of them are grounded in the tenets of psychological science and research.

This book is grounded in that science, and also filled with the kinds of stories that make for a compelling and interesting journey.

Despite my own solid self-esteem foundation, I learned more about self-esteem from this book than from any of my graduate school classes. And I learned that even a person with the poorest self-esteem will benefit from reading and participating in the exercises in this book. It is full of the kind of knowledge and wisdom that only a seasoned clinician like the author could provide.

Most importantly, I learned that the tools for enhancing and maintaining one's self-esteem are available to everyone, right now. All you need to do is make the decision to change, and stick to that decision every day from now on. I know it won't always be easy, but I trust that this book will be an invaluable guide to increasing your genuine self-esteem. Good luck in your journey!

—John M. Grohol, PsyD
    Founder and CEO, PsychCentral.com
    Newburyport, Massachusetts

Acknowledgments

In his book *Outliers*, Malcolm Gladwell argues that success in any endeavor comes from at least ten thousand hours of practice and then the luck of an opportunity coming our way. In my case, the two are intertwined. I am enormously grateful to John Grohol, CEO of PsychCentral.com, for giving me the opportunity to put in that ten thousand hours to develop my craft as a writer. Opportunity knocked again when I was contacted by acquisitions editor Wendy Millstine, of New Harbinger Publications, who had the patience and grace to support me through the proposal process. I owe many thanks to her as well as to her fellow acquisitions editor Jess O'Brien, editor Nicola Skidmore, and freelance copy editor Jasmine Star for their encouragement and helpful suggestions. Their thoughtful tutelage helped shape my thinking and my writing. The book is better for it.

But before the book, and before the writing, came a prior ten thousand plus hours dedicated to training and experience as a therapist and educator. For that I am deeply grateful to my very special teachers at the Alfred Adler Institute in Chicago: Robert L. Powers and Bronia Grunwald, whose words and example taught me to always look for people's strengths and encourage the growth that is their birthright. Over my thirty-five years of practice, I've done my best to honor their memories by doing exactly that. I am also grateful to my colleague Dan Tomasulo, who has generously shared his journey into positive psychology, and to the many pioneers in mind-body medicine whose work informs so much of what I do.

Finally, very special thanks to my family and friends, who have been there for me despite the benign neglect they experienced while I was working at both writing and a full-time job. Their love and collective support made this book possible.

INTRODUCTION

The Crisis of Self-Esteem

It's that awful awareness that nobody likes you, that you're not as good as other people, that you're a failure, a loser, a personal disaster; that you're ugly, or unintelligent, or don't have as much ability as someone else. It's that depressing feeling of worthlessness.

—James Dobson

I've been an online advice columnist for many years. Every day, I get letters from people who are in deep emotional pain. Many identify the problem as not having self-esteem or not having enough of it. Some are convinced that if they felt better about themselves, they'd do better in work or at school, have more friends, or find the love of their life. Mystified that others see them as successful, some feel bad about themselves and undeserving of the love and respect they get. The self-esteem of still others has taken such a hit because of bullying, failed efforts, or relationships gone bad that they've become immobilized by anxiety, depression, or both. Despite being reasonably attractive, intelligent, and decent human beings, their belief in themselves is unstable at best, and their ability to do what they need to do to meet their goals isn't what it should be.

Here are a few quotes from letters I've received. If you recognize yourself in any of them, you know how discouraged and down these people feel:

◊ "I am self-conscious about everything. I don't like my looks, my personality, or my background. Don't tell me to be myself. That's my problem. I don't want to be myself. I don't like me."—Forty-five-year-old woman

◊ "I know how to do a lot of things, but I don't have any self-esteem. I don't think I like myself very much. I don't think much of other people either."—Thirty-eight-year-old man

◊ "Please help me. My boyfriend left me kind of out of the blue. I'm devastated! I thought he was my best friend. How can I love myself when he doesn't love me?"—Twenty-two-year-old woman

◊ "Other people think I'm successful. I amaze everyone with what I do, but I'm constantly anxious. They don't know that all I can do when I get home is collapse."—Thirty-five-year-old woman

◊ "I can't settle on any career. Even though I was always in gifted programs in school, I've never felt good enough. I've already left two graduate programs, and I've quit a lot of jobs. Even thinking about what I should do next makes me so anxious and upset that I can't make a decision."—Twenty-four-year-old man

◊ "My parents always yell at me and tell me I'm stupid and ugly. My mom even said the saddest day of her life was when I was born. I don't do good in school and I'm fat. I don't have any friends really. I feel like self-harming and sometimes I'm suicidal. Maybe my mother is right that the world would be better without me?"—Fifteen-year-old girl

These people are all troubled and in trouble. None of them feel good about themselves. All of them lack a plan for changing it. Each is suffering from a crisis of self-esteem.

They are right to be concerned. Having positive self-esteem—believing that we are worthwhile people who are valued in our relationships and community—really is important. Positive self-esteem is central to people's ability to get up in the morning with some enthusiasm, to make and maintain positive relationships, to find a satisfying career, and to deal with the day-to-day problems of life. Without a solid positive sense of self, people start to feel depressed and helpless. If they feel like they're going through life faking it, they carry a deep underlying anxiety, worrying that others might see them as they think they really are and fearing that the good things in their life could vanish. Even if others see them as successful and happy, people with low self-esteem are constantly compensating for their feelings of being not quite good enough. It's exhausting. If you share any of those feelings, you know what it means to be in a crisis of self-esteem. If you've bought this book, you want to change it.

Like the people who write to me, you probably want to feel better about yourself. You may have bought into the idea that changing your feelings is the solution to your problems. While having positive self-esteem is crucial, you won't find it by focusing solely on a search for self-love. Why? Because the big "secret" of self-esteem is that feeling good is only half of the equation. It's also necessary to do things to deserve those good feelings. Paying attention to the *doing* can make all the difference.

This book broadens the definition of self-esteem to include both parts: feeling good and doing good, according to a sound system of personal values. I've named this two-part model of self-esteem *genuine self-esteem* to set it apart from the common idea that feelings are all that matter.

Here are the keys for unlocking your genuine self-esteem:

- Identifying and living by a strong, positive system of values (chapter 2)

- Paying attention to self-care (chapter 3)

- Developing the courage to act (chapter 4)

- Embracing a positive approach to life (chapter 5)

- Practicing mindfulness (chapter 6)

- Cultivating positive relationships (chapter 7)

By understanding and using these keys, we can all change our world for the better, and in so doing, change ourselves.

How to Use This Book

Gaining genuine self-esteem doesn't require you to follow a rigid, one-size-fits-all program. Instead, you can select from a broad menu of activities to create a plan that's specific to your unique needs. That's important. Research shows that we stay motivated when a plan fits our personality and needs (Sheldon and Lyubomirsky 2007). Self-assessments will help you analyze where the doing part of your self-esteem is fine and where it needs work.

You may find, for example, that you have more than enough courage to do the right thing for others but don't have enough positivity to take care of yourself. You might see that you're mindful about your experience when things are going well but need to build your circle of relationships to strengthen your support system. Then again, you may want to work on each key area not only because it never hurts to reinforce your strengths but because the activities can be fun.

In the final chapter, I've shared stories about how a few very different people have put together very individual plans to help themselves grow and change. You can do it too. I've also searched the Internet for sites that provide further information on topics in this book or that present the same information differently. I've compiled a list of Internet talks and animations to appeal to different learning styles, as well as recommended readings. This list of companion resources is available for download at http://www.newharbinger.com/31021. (See the back of the book for instructions on how to access the file.)

I encourage you to take your personal journey toward genuine self-esteem seriously. The pull of the familiar, even if it's negative and painful, is very powerful. If you want to turn your attitude toward yourself around, it's important to make a plan and commit to it for at least three months. Recent research indicates that the conventional idea that we can change a habit in twenty-eight days is a myth (Lally et al. 2010). Making significant change that will last is hard. You need at least a few months to undo old habits and put new ones in place. You wouldn't expect to lose twenty pounds by just reading about a diet. You wouldn't expect to heal a friendship after a fight by just thinking about it. You wouldn't expect to quit smoking through good intentions alone. Changing your self-esteem is no different. Change requires planned action. Take a leap of faith and give yourself the gift of a three-month plan. If you're suffering from a crisis of self-esteem, you deserve your own attention. Commit to your plan and you can change your life.

Each of us has the capacity to be creative and figure out what we need to do to grow. As Groucho Marx is reputed to have said, "Each morning when I open my eyes, I say to myself, 'I, not events, have the power to make me happy or unhappy today. I can choose which it shall be. Yesterday is dead, tomorrow hasn't arrived yet. I have just one day, today, and I'm going to be happy in it'" (Bannink 2012, 16).

CHAPTER 1

The Definition
of Self-Esteem
Is the Problem

Self-esteem is not a free gift of nature. It has to be cultivated—has to be earned.

—Nathaniel Branden

I f you've been doing your best to fix your self-esteem with little success, the problem may not be a lack of effort, sincerity, or willingness on your part. For many people who are in search of better self-esteem, the problem lies not in their efforts but in their definition of "self-esteem." Yes, the definition. How we define things determines how we think about them and what we think we need to do. If our definitions are wrong, even good efforts won't produce good results. For the last forty or fifty years, the definition of self-esteem as accepted by the popular culture has been inaccurate and unhelpful. At least in the United States, that definition has been that "self-esteem" means feeling positive and good about yourself.

While researching this book, I came across an astounding study that reviewed fifteen thousand studies of self-esteem and its relevance to succeeding in, well, just about anything

(Baumeister et al. 2003). As it turned out, all but two hundred of those studies were flawed in methodology or conclusions. Even that smaller group didn't demonstrate that having high self-esteem, defined as feelings of positive self-worth, did anything to improve people's grades, success, leadership potential, friendships, or love life. Further, high positive self-regard doesn't prevent kids from cheating, stealing, bullying, or experimenting with drugs. At the time, the lead author of the review study was quoted as saying that his findings were the biggest disappointment of his career (Bronson and Merryman 2009).

The Two-Part Definition: A New Place to Start

While popular psychology has focused on feeling good as the antidote to low self-esteem, researchers have been doing what researchers do. They've asked, "If feeling good doesn't help people live well, what does?" What they've discovered is really a rediscovery of what some philosophers and psychologists knew as far back as the nineteenth century: that people need more than positive feelings about themselves to be psychologically healthy and have positive connections with others. Those feelings have to be grounded in being a decent person who lives decently.

The social scientists and psychologists who have been pursuing this idea have given it many names: the dual model of self-esteem (Franks and Marolla 1976), the two-factor theory (Tafarodi and Swann Jr. 1995), the multidimensional approach (O'Brien and Epstein 1983), and authentic self-esteem (Mruk 2013), to cite only a few. I'm calling it genuine self-esteem in recognition of the truth that underlies all of those terms, and to separate it from the inaccurate model that limits the definition to loving oneself.

What the dual models all have in common is the belief that living a good life hinges on both feeling good about yourself and doing good things to deserve it. Why? Because if we stick to just *feeling* good without *doing* good, even a lowlife can have high self-esteem. Criminals can feel very good about themselves for doing what they do, especially if they get away with it. The same is true of philanderers and sociopaths. Further, feeling good about oneself as a result of doing bad things, such as putting other people down, bullying, lying, cheating, hurting people, or accomplishing things at others' expense, doesn't count. A healthy feeling of positive self-regard must be based on doing things that contribute to the greater good in our relationships and in our community.

Genuine self-esteem reasserts the connection between feeling good about yourself and doing good things to earn that positive self-regard. The two parts are in constant interaction with each other, as illustrated in the following figure.

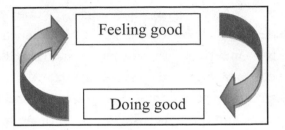

"Doing good" has a wonderful double meaning. It can mean "I'm doing good" as in "I'm fine," or it can mean "I'm doing good" as in "I'm a person who does charitable, moral things." The two-part definition of self-esteem embraces both meanings of the phrase. It reflects the conviction that people who do good things for themselves and others are people who feel fine and do well in life.

People knew this as long ago as the ancient Greeks. Aristotle's golden mean says that we must act for the right reasons and with the right feelings. The researchers previously cited, who are writing about the two-part model of self-esteem, agree. They know that merely sitting around feeling good about ourselves doesn't add up to much. So why hasn't the two-part definition taken hold?

Well, let's face it: as a cultural group, Americans like things to be fast and easy. Our culture likes fast food, fast cars, drive-up windows, and brief psychotherapy. If a pill or surgery can fix something, why sign on for weeks or months of steady work? Fixing self-esteem by saying "I love you" to a mirror three times a day fits right into the desire for a quick and simple solution. I have to admit that there's a part of me that truly wishes I could just think positive thoughts or take a pill to be more fit, more organized, more successful, and even more worthy of love.

But here's the apparent contradiction in the American psyche: we also deeply admire people who are team players, who are everyday heroes making a difference, and who live their lives with integrity. I think that's what the flap over steroid use in sports is about. The athletes who resort to performance-enhancing drugs as an easy way to succeed betray our sense of what is heroic or right. That, along with their denials, offends our sense of what is fair and decent.

The two-part definition of genuine self-esteem appeals to both aspects of most people's values system. Yes, we want and need to feel good about ourselves. But we also need to do things in a way that's good. The two are in a constant loop. Doing good makes us feel good about ourselves, which gives us the positive energy to do good, which makes us feel better about ourselves, which further enhances our ability to do good things. You get the idea.

But what does it mean to do "good" as in what's "right," "moral," or "fair"? That suggests a values system that includes ideas about what is ethical and beneficial in the wider world, beyond oneself. From early- to mid-twentieth-century psychologists like Alfred Adler and Carl Rogers to more recent developers of positive psychology like Martin Seligman and Barbara Fredrickson, there is a shared assumption that, in our hearts, we all know what is fair and right and helpful to self and others, and that it is basic to being human to want to contribute and grow in our community. Worthiness—actually doing things that are worthy of admiration and respect—may be an old-fashioned concept, but it's still central to being a good partner, a good parent, a good friend, and a positive member of any team, work group, or community. Being "worthy" or "good" means being honest, trustworthy, and decent. It means understanding that we and others have value and that everyone deserves to be treated equally and with respect.

This doesn't require following a particular religion or spiritual practice, although this often helps people develop a more certain personal code of ethics. It is assumed that to be human means we all start off instinctively humanistic, striving for mutual respect and caring. We make good decisions about life choices because we generally know what's good for ourselves and the people around us. (We'll take a closer look at values and how we develop them in chapter 2.)

Of course, even very good people can sometimes do bad things. But bad decisions—defined as decisions that are selfish and hurt others, that are unethical, or that set us back—usually don't come from wanting to do bad things. They usually come from not knowing all the facts, not understanding the consequences of a choice, or not having enough personal strength to withstand others' negative opinions about a choice we made that was good, right, and fair. Everyone is entitled to make mistakes in this complicated thing called life. As soon as we see that we've been hurtful, most of us don't feel very good about ourselves. Then the challenge is to recognize the error and find a way to make it right. When we do, our self-esteem comes back into balance.

Remember, the two-part definition of genuine self-esteem can be summarized by this equation:

Genuine self-esteem = feeling good + doing good

Where We Are Now

Currently, I see three important factors at work regarding self-esteem. First, as often happens, the pendulum had to swing too far before it could settle down. Swing it did. At one end of the arc is the American focus prior to the 1950s that emphasized conformity, duty, and an authoritarian approach to parenting and discipline. The emphasis then was on doing what was right. It didn't matter how you felt about it or how you felt about yourself. In reaction, the pendulum swung to the assumption found in over 5,500 self-esteem books currently available—books that emphasize the importance of feeling good about yourself—that a sense of individual specialness is the key to success, achievement, and happiness. In the process of that swing, the other, equally important part of self-esteem, the "doing good" part, was forgotten or minimized. We lost sight of the fact that positive self-esteem has to include doing what's right for oneself and others.

Second, the rise of positive psychology since the 1990s has created space for reconsidering what developing our self-esteem really requires. This is allowing for a paradigm shift from an emphasis on self-involvement to a focus on the importance of positive engagement with life. As Martin Seligman (who is generally credited as the father of positive psychology) stated, "There is no question that feeling high self-esteem is a delightful state to be in, but trying to achieve the feeling side of self-esteem directly, before achieving good commerce with the world, confuses profoundly the means and the end" (2007, 33). When he speaks of "commerce," he isn't referring to making money—although that can certainly be part of it. Commerce, in this sense, means positive social interactions.

Finally, the pendulum is settling down. From expectations of suffering and duty on one end to expectations of happiness through self-absorption on the other, we are now moving to an understanding that both feeling good and doing good are required for a good life. From the idea that children should be seen and not heard to the idea that children should never be squelched, we're moving to a balanced view that kids (and, indeed, we adults) need to value themselves but also have and follow a system of values that help them live in good ways. It takes both—feeling good and doing good—to create a happy and successful life. It requires having strong positive values and being willing to correct ourselves when we don't stay true to them.

Self-Esteem Self-Assessment

Are you in a crisis of self-esteem? The following self-assessment will help you determine where you are now on the two sides of the self-esteem equation, feeling and doing. Read through the following statements and check off all that apply to you. Don't think too hard about it; just go with your first impression.

_____ 1. I'm constantly hard on myself.

_____ 2. I'm often confused about what would be fair in a situation.

_____ 3. I'm always comparing myself negatively to others.

_____ 4. I don't think I have what it takes to recover from a tragedy. I wouldn't know where to start.

_____ 5. I don't feel very good about myself.

_____ 6. I don't think I have much to offer the world.

_____ 7. I frequently feel like I'm so different from others that I'll never fit in.

_____ 8. I don't know what to do with my life.

_____ 9. I really wish I were somebody else.

_____ 10. It's better to stay home or in my room than to be with other people.

_____ 11. I worry that others will find out I'm not as good at doing things as they think I am.

_____ 12. There's no point to setting goals. I'll never come close to achieving them.

_____ 13. I self-harm or think about suicide because I know I'll never amount to much.

_____ 14. I can't help anyone else. It's all I can do to take care of myself.

_____ 15. I don't think I'm very important.

_____ 16. I think it's better to keep my opinions about social issues to myself.

_____ 17. I don't understand what my partner sees in me.

_____ 18. I don't give it my all at school or work because I don't see the point.

_____ 19. I don't think I'm worthy of respect.

_____ 20. I'm not a joiner.

_____ 21. I don't think I'm smart enough to make good decisions.

_____ 22. I'm often paralyzed when it will take some risk to accomplish something I want to do.

Scoring

Checked items with odd numbers are indicators of a shaky self-liking. You're not feeling good enough.

Checked items with even numbers are indicators that you've backed away from life. You're not doing good enough.

If you checked off more than a few items on the assessment (say, more than five), it confirms what you probably already know about yourself: your genuine self-esteem needs work—maybe quite a bit of work. I don't have to tell you how self-esteem issues play out in your life. Your life isn't working as you believe it should. You may be self-critical and anxious about being criticized by others. You may be pessimistic and depressed about your ability to handle the daily problems of life or make positive connections with others. The things you've already tried in an effort to help yourself function and be happy haven't done the job.

Here's the good news: You've already begun doing what it takes to improve your genuine self-esteem. You've opened this book and read this far. That means you have some hope that you can make things better. And it means you're willing to take another chance at building or rebuilding your positive sense of self. That's already progress. That tells me that you have at least a bit of solid emotional ground to stand on. We can build from there.

Understanding the Two-Part Definition of Self-Esteem

The following grid illustrates how the relationship between the two parts of genuine self-esteem can impact a person's life.

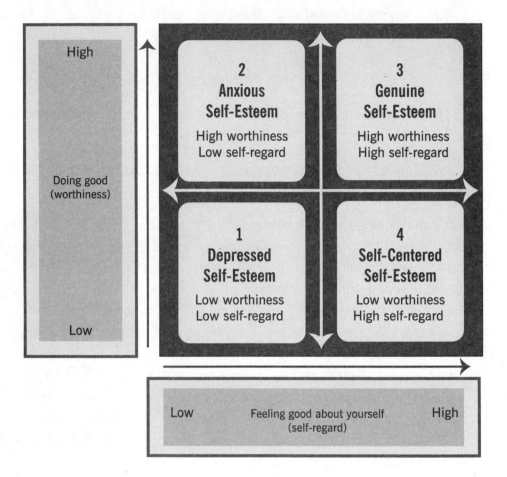

The bottom line (from left to right) rates how you're *feeling* about yourself. It ranges from feeling terrible about yourself to feeling great about who you are. The line on the left side (from bottom to top) reflects how well you're *doing* in terms of using positive values to do good things in life. It ranges from a low of seldom doing what's worthy, right, and principled to a high of regularly doing what's worthy, right, and principled.

The healthiest, most productive spot to be in is quadrant 3. People in that quadrant have genuine self-esteem. They have a strong sense of self-worth and a well-developed sense of what's right and fair (values) that they regularly put into action. That's what we're all aiming for. If you aren't solidly in quadrant 3 most of the time, you probably experience yourself as having shaky or low self-esteem.

The other three quadrants are often emotionally draining, though for different reasons. People who find themselves in any of those quadrants most of the time can benefit from projects like the ones outlined in this book to help them move toward living life in quadrant 3, genuine self-esteem, more often.

Of course, with life being what it is, spending more time in quadrant 3 isn't really that simple. How we feel about ourselves (self-regard) and how we act in terms of making good and right choices (being worthy) can vary from situation to situation. We all have times and situations when we move from one quadrant to another. When that happens, the degree of damage to our overall genuine self-esteem depends on how much the situation means to us and how often we find ourselves there. A visit to one of the other quadrants can be just that—a visit. It need not affect your general evaluation of yourself as someone who is a good person with solid, genuine self-esteem.

Let's use my client Jane as an example. Now thirty years old, she was raised in a highly dysfunctional family. Her parents have been verbally and sometimes physically abusive for as long as she can remember. Yet she's a generous friend and a loving partner and mother, despite her difficult upbringing. She has a belief that she should visit her parents more often and should find a way to love them, but her efforts haven't paid off. For her, abandoning the toxic relationship is healthy. She can't continue to hang her sense of worthiness as a person on her inability to create a loving relationship with her unloving parents. Even though doing so would mean a lot to her, and even though she's tried as best she can, continuing to work on connecting with her parents and hoping to change them would only hurt her further—and probably annoy or even outrage her parents. So she gave up trying, in spite of her values in regard to the importance of connection to family. She still feels bad about this sometimes, but generally she can leave her "shoulds" in quadrant 1 with only a little regret.

Before we take a close look at quadrant 3, let's take a tour of the other three parts of the grid. Although it may seem that quadrants 1, 2, and 4 are solely problematic, there can be healthy ways to visit each one.

Quadrant 1: Depressed Self-Esteem

Let's begin with quadrant 1, depressed self-esteem, defined by a low sense of worthiness and low self-regard.

1
**Depressed
Self-Esteem**

Low worthiness
Low self-regard

Unhealthy Quadrant 1

People who tend to be stuck in quadrant 1 have a more general difficulty interacting posi-tively with the world and don't feel very good about themselves. If they're stuck in quadrant 1, they often feel depressed. And if they get stuck there too long about too many things, they may become suicidal. Sadly, people in this situation don't like themselves very much and don't believe they can handle problems in a principled way or maintain relationships that are based on mutual respect. Those who are in school don't believe they can be successful and may decide that they don't really value getting an education. They may stop attending class and doing assignments. Those who are in the workforce may have a feeling that they're the weak link and feel unsure about how they can change that. Instead of consulting with someone about how they might improve, they tell themselves that they don't care. In relationships, they may feel undeserving of good treatment. Overall, they may find that it's easier to back away from life's difficulties, thinking it's better not to try than to fail again. That strategy can lower stress, but it also eliminates the opportunity to grow, since growth only comes from struggling with a challenge and mastering it.

> Twisy is typical of someone who's stuck in quadrant 1. "I'm a loser," she told me. "I feel like I'm a waste of space and time. I don't like my job much, and I don't see any future in it. I can do it okay, but it looks like I'll be doing the same thing at fifty that I'm doing at twenty-five. The only reason I'm not suicidal is that I'm scared I'd blow that too." When I asked her if we could think about ways she might improve her situation, she replied that she is too depressed, it's too hard, and her boss probably wouldn't let her do anything different anyway. She assumes there's nothing she can do to positively impact her job or feel better about herself.

Healthy Quadrant 1

A visit to healthy quadrant 1 is when, like Jane in the example I gave, you make a decision that an issue isn't all that important to you or will only hurt you or others if you pursue it. This often involves being willing to feel a little sad and apologetic, and maybe even somewhat guilty, for opting out. In fact, those guilty feelings help us maintain our personal values system. If we don't want to keep trying to fix something that's important but hopeless, the least we can do is feel a little guilty about it. That lets us and others know that our values system is intact. If we had it our way, we would probably keep trying to do better, but changing some situations is beyond our control, or the price for trying is too high.

Quadrant 2: Anxious Self-Esteem

Quadrant 2, anxious self-esteem, is defined by a high sense of worthiness coupled with low self-regard. In some situations, that isn't as contradictory as it may seem.

Unhealthy Quadrant 2

Folks who are generally stuck in quadrant 2 can look very successful, but they're constantly anxious. Their self-esteem is built entirely on being the best and the brightest: the most creative, innovative, smart, or whatever "most" they think they should be, especially in comparison to other people. People who live in this quadrant most of the time think it's not enough to be good at what they do. To feel secure, they feel they have to be better than others. Sometimes they may even be willing to behave less than honorably to get and keep that top spot. Therefore, their self-esteem is often only as high as their most recent accomplishment. It's exhausting. They aren't working from a position of principle—of doing good or being good.

They're mainly concerned with *looking* good. Like the wizard in the original *Wizard of Oz* movie, they don't want people to draw back the curtain and see them as they really are.

To defend themselves from falling down a notch in comparison to others, people who are stuck in quadrant 2 are often competitive and controlling. Many have affairs to prove their attractiveness to themselves. They may even try to pull someone away from another romantic relationship just to prove they can. Often enough, they then lose interest, much to the confusion and misery of the person who thought she or he was loved. Many neglect family life in favor of activities where results are more measurable. Sadly, their strategies for feeling good about themselves often backfire. People who are constantly striving to be better than others generally aren't well liked or respected. If you've ever compromised your positive values or fallen into any of these poor choices, you know how anxiety provoking this way of life can be.

> Angeles quickly rose to the top of her company's engineering team, but she's so focused on being the best that she's lost sight of what it takes to be a team player. (If you saw the movie *The Heat*, you'll recognize this kind of person in Sandra Bullock's character.) She's confused that her teammates don't invite her along when they go out after work. "I work hard," she told me. "I get the job done. Why don't people appreciate me?" It's simple: her need to be superior to other people in order to feel secure shows. Yes, she's highly competent, but she can never let herself enjoy it. She's too bent on being better.

Healthy Quadrant 2

I'll use myself as an example of visiting quadrant 2 in a healthy way. I often do public speaking; I'm told I'm very good at it. It matters to me that I do a good job for the people who have asked me to speak. But one of my not-so-carefully kept secrets is that I'm always anxious before I get up in front of people. That little bit of uncertainty about whether I can do what I mean to do actually keeps me on my game. It helps me do my best. Many actors feel the same way. They see a little stage fright as a good thing. During a recent TV special on the remaking of *The Sound of Music*, a reporter asked Carrie Underwood if she were nervous. She replied, "I think being nervous is kind of good. If you're not nervous, if you're not getting butterflies, it might mean you don't care" (Underwood 2013). None of us nervous public speakers are focused on what other people think. We use our sense of being not quite good enough and feeling bad about it to push ourselves to do the job well. As long as our feelings of uncertainty are limited to a few areas or are actually helpful, our overall sense of being in quadrant 3 isn't damaged.

Quadrant 4: Self-Centered Self-Esteem

I'm going to skip to quadrant 4 to discuss the last "nongenuine" quadrant before getting to the ideal spot. We'll get back to quadrant 3 in a minute. I promise. Quadrant 4, self-centered self-esteem, is characterized by a low sense of worthiness but a high sense of self-regard. As with quadrant 2, this isn't as contradictory as it may seem.

4
Self-Centered
Self-Esteem

Low worthiness
High self-regard

Unhealthy Quadrant 4

People who live in quadrant 4 most of the time have high positive self-regard coupled with a generally low opinion of others and disrespect for social rules. They've become very self-centered. They have an ego as big as Texas, and they don't understand it when others don't agree that they're special—or even spectacular. Yet underneath all that superior behavior lie profound feelings of inferiority. Deep inside, such people usually know they don't have what it takes to be worthy of others' respect. They therefore may shore themselves up with exaggerations of their contributions and abilities and an arrogant attitude. Their relationships last only as long as others are willing to admire them without questioning their decisions or positive opinions about themselves. They sometimes develop narcissistic personality disorder. They may have become so adept at lying about their worth that they actually believe their own lies, in which case they wouldn't recognize themselves if they read this. I have enormous sympathy for such people. This is a very hard way to live.

> Louis is a prime example of someone with narcissistic personality disorder. He always has something negative to say about other people and tries to make himself look good by claiming that he's superior. He's a nightmare to work for since he inflates any of his accomplishments and takes credit for the work of his employees. He remains friends with people only as long as they admire him. His girlfriend hangs on his every word, feeding his ego.

Meanwhile, everyone else wonders what she sees in him. Yes, he's gorgeous, but...really? If anyone questions Louis's high self-estimation, he gets very defensive and may go on the attack. If he can't be the best, he tells himself, at least he's better than everyone else.

Healthy Quadrant 4

There are times when we don't know how to be principled but still feel positively about ourselves. Sometimes these situations are dilemmas that push us to learn. Feeling worthwhile enough to ask for help and do one's best to find an ethical and positive way to solve a problem can take a person to a new and important place. For example, if I feel positively about myself and life hands me a big problem I can't solve in ways that I feel are ethical and respectful, my general sense of myself as a worthwhile person can help me persevere.

Quadrant 3: Genuine Self-Esteem

This brings us to quadrant 3: genuine self-esteem. Ta-da! This is where we all want to be most of the time. Genuine self-esteem is characterized by high positive self-regard that's earned by handling life ethically and connecting with others positively. People who live here most of the time have a general sense that they're worthwhile, decent people who have what it takes to manage life in a principled way. Although you've bought this book, you may be pleasantly surprised to find that you already have more genuine self-esteem than you thought you had!

3
Genuine
Self-Esteem

High worthiness
High self-regard

People with genuine self-esteem don't have to be the best. Their positive values system and high regard for other people let them be team players, surviving and thriving in the process. When there's a decision to make, they typically do what's right and fair. They're self-confident without being overbearing, and they share the limelight when they achieve a goal. Their lives aren't filled with stress and drama. Instead, their level of emotion is generally proportional to the situation.

We see folks with genuine self-esteem on the news every time there's a natural disaster like a hurricane or tornado. Their house has been reduced to sticks, but they say, "Well, what counts is that my family and neighbors survived. Stuff is just stuff. We'll be okay." Their sense of worth is built on their connections to people and on a values system that gives them a way to work through the most difficult of times.

If you live in quadrant 3, one of your strengths is that you're willing to reach for help when you need it. You don't need to know all the answers to feel good about yourself. It doesn't diminish your sense of personal value to ask for assistance and accept it. If I were to see you in therapy, it would be to support you and to help you figure out what to do next in a difficult situation that challenges your values in a new or major way. These are times that require us to dig deep and find the courage to be true to our basic values in spite of other costs. Have no doubt about it: even people in quadrant 3 can get overwhelmed, upset, and indecisive when life throws them a big challenge to their genuine self-esteem.

> Vicky is squarely in quadrant 3. She came to therapy after the sudden death of her husband when a driver who was asleep at the wheel hit him head-on. Left with two small children, she was overwhelmed with her grief and everything she had to do. I soon learned that working with her meant getting out of her way. She didn't need therapy so much as she needed a supportive sounding board. Therapy, she told me, was a place where she could talk about her difficulties without guilt. Even though she had lots of support from family and friends, she didn't want to burn them out with her many problems. Although I did occasionally offer a suggestion, mostly I saw myself as a benevolent witness to her process of putting her life back together. Within a few months, she made the practical adjustments and arrangements she needed to make while still acknowledging her enormous loss and honoring the memory of her husband, the love of her life. Yes, she was still grieving, but she managed to create a reasonable, values-based life for herself and her children that would eventually let them move on.

Taking Stock of Your Level of Self-Esteem

This exercise will help you take a look at how much time you spend in each of the self-esteem quadrants.

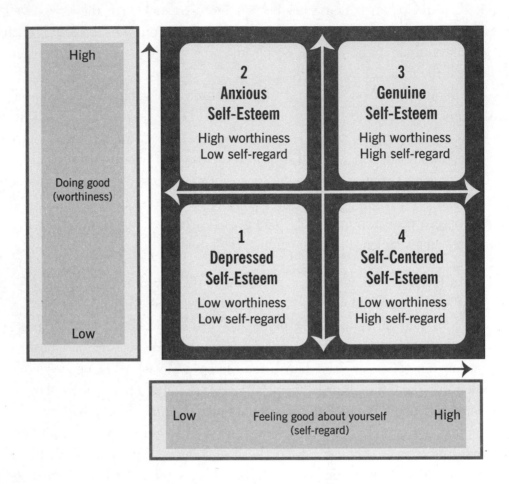

Put a star in the quadrant you think you live in most of the time.

Most people primarily inhabit one quadrant but can identify parts of their lives and specific situations in which they visit the others. Although your aim is to be in quadrant 3 most of the time, it's okay to find yourself in the other quadrants in certain situations if you can do that in a healthy way.

Now take some time to think about any areas of life where you find yourself in quadrants 1, 2, or 4 in healthy ways. Later, we'll consider unhealthy aspects of your life that you might want to work on. For now, though, let's identify your strengths. These are the foundation for heightening your genuine self-esteem.

Quadrant 1. List areas in your life where you sometimes feel you should do better and feel kind of sad and guilty that you don't. These might be things that, for the sake of your mental health, you've given up on as hopeless.

_____

_____

_____

Quadrant 2. List areas of life in which you have high values and principled expectations for yourself but don't quite perform to your own expectations—or don't give yourself enough credit.

_____

_____

_____

Quadrant 4. List areas of life where you don't yet have enough clarity about your values but still feel fine about yourself.

_____

_____

_____

You probably live in quadrant 3 a good deal of the time, even if you don't think you do. Take a moment now to list at least five areas of your life in which you are acting from a strong and positive values system and in which you feel positive about yourself:

1. _____

2. _____

3. _____

4. _____

5. _____

6. Bonus: *I have the courage and motivation to increase my sense of worthiness and self-regard by working with this book.*

Let's Review

Doing better in just about any aspect of life lies in using the two-part definition of self-esteem: feeling good by doing good. People who are high in both parts of the definition are high on life. They tend to be happier, more successful, and more fulfilled than those who emphasize only one or the other part of the equation. They have the courage and perseverance to deal with life's challenges, and they understand that feeling positive about themselves requires having positive values and being positively connected to others. They also understand that life is indeed very complicated, so they cut themselves and others some slack at times when they aren't able to live entirely in quadrant 3.

If you already live in quadrant 3 of the self-esteem grid most of the time, this book will help you validate and reinforce your healthy genuine self-esteem. If you find yourself in the other quadrants more than you think is healthy for you, you have some work to do. This book will show you the way.

CHAPTER 2

Values: Where the "Good" in "Doing Good" Comes From

My secret agenda is to convey my values to my kids.

—Robert Fulghum

Our values are our very personal frames of reference for what's good, right, and worthwhile. They vary depending on a person's culture, religion, and upbringing. Once internalized, they become guideposts for how to live a worthwhile life. When we live up to them, we feel good about ourselves. When we feel good about ourselves, we have the motivation and strength to further follow our convictions about what's right. That's what it means to have genuine self-esteem.

The "doing good" part of genuine self-esteem comes from consistently making decisions based on our personal system of values. But we can't stand up for what we believe in unless we know where we stand. This chapter will help you think about where your values come from and how you've incorporated your experiences into a personal code of ethics. Exercises later in this chapter will help you more clearly define the values system that guides you.

Your values are derived from a number of sources. Here are some of the primary influences:

◊ Your family

◊ Benevolent witnesses

◊ Fictional heroes and media figures

◊ The times you live in

◊ Self-esteem dilemmas

They've been formed, confirmed, or challenged from the minute you were born until the minute you're reading this sentence. Let's take a brief look at each of these factors and how they may have influenced the formation of your personal moral road map for life.

Values Derived from Family

It all starts at the beginning. Having supportive parents who have positive values and the ability, time, and attention to provide a loving home is the best prescription for growing up with solid genuine self-esteem. Such parents talk the talk and walk the walk. They live and teach honesty, integrity, altruism, and respect for others. Such parents don't need to deliberately instill values into their children. Their values are transmitted in hundreds of everyday ways.

Think about it: young children who are still in the process of becoming socialized have tantrums, refuse to share, put things in their mouths and noses that they shouldn't, and sometimes ask question that make their parents wish the earth would open up and swallow them. "Why is that lady fat?" they might innocently ask, or "What's the matter with his nose?" The kids aren't being rude. They're exploring, learning, and growing.

How parents, older siblings, and other relatives react transforms the child's experiences into a values system. When grown-ups applaud and give out rewards in the form of hugs, smiles, and even treats, kids are likely to bask in the attention and do whatever it was again and again. When the grown-ups who care for them withdraw their attention and warmth, kids learn that doing whatever it was wasn't such a good idea. A clear scolding that a child is being a bad girl by calling her grandma ugly, or being told in no uncertain terms that grabbing a toy away from a little brother hurts his feelings, lets a child know not to do that again.

It's through hundreds and thousands of events like these—both major and minor—that we form our system of values and notions of what's good, fair, and right. Robert Fulghum's 1988 essay "All I Really Need to Know I Learned in Kindergarten" (share everything, play fair, don't hit people, and so on) resonates with people because it highlights the values we want all children to learn, along with reading and writing and brushing their teeth.

Benevolent Witnesses

Unfortunately, not every kid gets the family and home life he or she deserves. Kids who are hungry for safety and good values often start hanging out at the home of a friend who has a more supportive family. Others find excuses to stay after school with a favorite teacher or become the right-hand helpers of a coach, art teacher, or youth group leader so they can linger in the gym, art room, or meeting room. They probably think they're volunteering to straighten up the room and just chatting with an adult who likes them. They may not realize that they've found a way to straighten out their values in the process. The adults these kids seek out—people who offer alternative positive adult role models—are sometimes referred to as benevolent witnesses.

Some kids are creative and find a benevolent witness or source of goodness in their imagination, in a house of worship, or in nature. One of my teachers used to share a case of a little girl who lived with a harsh grandmother who only fed her on weekends, when other relatives came to visit. The child decided that sunbeams were her deceased parents, shining love to her. It helped her bear the mistreatment and hold on to the positive values her parents had taught her before they died in a tragic accident. When she grew up, she became a social worker so she could help other deprived kids survive and thrive.

Identifying Family Members Who Influenced Your Values

The foundation for our individual values system comes from our original family, however family was defined. As we grow, we accept some of those values and embrace them as our own. Who were the important family role models in your early years? Think about older siblings and other relatives as well as parent figures.

_____

_____

_____

Identifying Benevolent Witnesses Who Influenced Your Values

If you weren't born into a positive, nurturing family, or if there were other important older role models in your life, who were your benevolent witnesses? Youth leaders? Other adults? God? A positive imaginary friend? List your role models here:

_____

_____

_____

Values Formed in Reaction to Upbringing

Sometimes our values are a reaction to how we were raised. When we see that some values create conflict, pain, or trouble, we start to sort them into those we'll keep and those we won't. In some cases, we even decide to take an entirely opposite point of view.

> Jacqui's values are a typical combination of acceptance and rejection of family values. She came from a family that was chaotic. Her overworked and overwhelmed single mother made it clear that Jacqui and her three sisters were expected to be independent and strong and not ask for much attention. The girls were certain they were loved, and they were also clear that the best way to get their mother's approval was to take care of their own problems. Jacqui values personal independence and strength, which were strong values in her family. But she doesn't want to repeat the distance and the "everyone on their own" feeling. She wants her kids to have more hugs, closeness, and connection. Therefore, she makes certain that the family gets together for dinner every night, and that they celebrate anything that can be celebrated. She also makes sure she has time to have a quiet chat with each of her kids every evening and to read aloud to them before bedtime.

Identifying Values You Developed in Reaction to Your Upbringing

Are there values from your family of origin that you swore you wouldn't repeat? For example, as I was growing up, my family highly valued conformity almost no matter what. As an adult, I've been thoughtful about when it's wise to conform and when it's better to march to a different drummer. Take some time to think about whether some of your values are a reflection of your effort to live life differently from how you were raised. Now note any values you've rejected and those you've adopted instead.

Value I've rejected: _____

What I value instead: _____

Value I've rejected: _____

What I value instead: _____

Value I've rejected: _____

What I value instead: _____

Value I've rejected: _____

What I value instead: _____

Fictional Heroes and Celebrities

When adult role models are absent or unsupportive, some children and young people look to the movies, novels, or even video games to figure out how to live a better life. More than a few of my students at a local college come from backgrounds filled with violence, both on the street and at home. For them, stories of fictional characters or historical figures who were able to change their lives served as beacons of hope and provided guidance for choosing healthier values than what they saw in action every day.

> Tremaine grew up in a city neighborhood where gangs ruled. His father was a brutal alcoholic. His mother kept a low profile as she tried to keep her family together. I asked Tremaine how he managed to get himself to

college. He said, "When I was younger, my teachers saw I was smart. I'd finish my work before everyone else, so they'd send me to the library. Early on, a librarian showed me a shelf of biographies of famous people. Lots of them didn't have it so good when they were young either. I figured if they could make something of themselves, I could too." He studied hard and got a full scholarship to college.

Identifying Values Derived from Fictional Heroes and Celebrities

Don't underestimate the importance of fictional heroes and celebrities in informing your values. These role models, whether in sports, entertainment, movies, films, or books, can have an enormous influence on growing minds. Do you still remember any such role models from your childhood? Who were they and what did they stand for?

Hero: _____

What this hero stood for that I've adopted for myself: _____

_____

Hero: _____

What this hero stood for that I've adopted for myself: _____

_____

Hero: _____

What this hero stood for that I've adopted for myself: _____

_____

Hero: _____

What this hero stood for that I've adopted for myself: _____

_____

The Times We Live In

Another factor that influences our personal values system is the historical and cultural context we're raised in. Therefore, understanding a little history is important if we are to understand ourselves. Our efforts to define our values and, indeed, our identity occur in the context of something much bigger than our family of origin, a childhood neighborhood, or early heroes. We are also products of our generation.

National and local events, social changes, and even the music that was important to us as we grew into adulthood have profound effects on us and who we become. As a result, we tend to share at least some values or aspects of our worldview with those who grew up at the same time. (Incidentally, this is one of the reasons why people rarely get into relationships with people ten or more years older or younger than they are. Once there is an age difference of a decade, people often don't share cultural reference points or values.)

Below, I briefly outline key influences on each generation as shared by the likely readership of this book. Of course, it is by definition quite general, especially because cultural influences continue to change and evolve during the time span experienced by each generation. However, the information presented below does provide a glimpse of representative cultural influences that were prominent in the United States as each group reached young adulthood. If you were born near the dividing line between two generations, you may share values with people from both adjoining generations. Those who were actively involved in cultural movements are likely to have experienced the same years differently from those who (by circumstance or lack of interest) were not. Nevertheless, there is some conventional agreement about the general spirit of the times that was experienced by each generation.

Silent Generation: Born 1925–1945.

Key events and social movements: Roaring Twenties, the Great Depression, World War II, the Korean War, the G.I. Bill, postwar recovery, the Cold War, the Red Scare, the polio epidemic.

Home entertainment: In the early years, no TV. Families gathered around the radio for shows such as *Arthur Godfrey Time*, *The Shadow*, *You Are There*, *The Amateur Hour*, and *The Abbott and Costello Show*. A later group saw the introduction of television.

Communications: Letters and telephone. Many people had a party phone line at first.

Technology: No computers.

Popular music: Big band, swing, Tommy Dorsey, Frank Sinatra, Buddy Holly, Nat King Cole, Louis Armstrong.

Diversity: General acceptance of racial, gender, and class barriers.

Parenting styles: Autocratic. During the depression, kids often worked at adult jobs.

Ethics as people came to adulthood: A clear moral code based on doing the right thing.

Youth attitude: Follow the rules.

Baby Boomers: Born 1946–1964.

Key events and social movements: The postwar economic boom, the Space Race, the Vietnam War, the Summer of Love, the Kent State shootings, the civil rights movement, communes, feminism, Watergate, the assassinations of JFK, RFK, and MLK.

Home entertainment: TV in most homes, with everyone in the family watching the same thing at the same time—shows such as *The Adventures of Ozzie and Harriet, Father Knows Best, The Mickey Mouse Club, Bonanza, Star Trek, The Andy Griffith Show, Route 66,* and *All in the Family.*

Communications: Letters and one phone line per household with extension phones in different rooms.

Technology: Computers as big as buildings.

Popular music: Folk music, rock and roll, disco, Motown, Elvis Presley, Pete Seeger, Diana Ross, the Beatles, Elton John.

Diversity: Breaking down barriers between races, genders, and classes.

Parenting styles: Autocratic and hierarchical, with Dr. Spock shaking things up in later years.

Ethics as people came to adulthood: Situational ethics based on feeling good. The human potential movement begins.

Youth attitude: Question the rules.

Generation X: Born 1965–1984.

Key events and social movements: Three Mile Island, the Iran hostage crisis, the assassination of John Lennon, the AIDS epidemic, the Columbine High School massacre, escalating divorce rate, economic downturn, terrorism, global warming, the dot-com bubble and bust.

Home entertainment: VCRs and video stores. Popular TV shows included *The Brady Bunch, The Partridge Family, Sesame Street, Gilligan's Island, Donnie and Marie, Star Trek: The Next Generation, Seinfeld, MASH,* and *The Cosby Show.*

Communications: Cell phones and e-mail.

Technology: Desktop computers.

Popular music: Heavy metal, hip-hop, R&B, Billy Joel, Madonna, Whitney Houston, Bruce Springsteen, Phil Collins, Alanis Morissette.

Diversity: Acceptance of diversity.

Parenting styles: Democratic parenting. Everyone gets a trophy.

Ethics as people came to adulthood: Entitlement, but also the rise of more involvement in service activity.

Youth attitude: Reject the rules.

Millennials: Born 1985–2004.

Key events and social movements: The September 11th attacks, the Iraq and Afghanistan wars, LGBT rights, the financial crisis of 2007–2008, school and mall shootings, increasing numbers of natural disasters.

Home entertainment: On-demand TV and streaming video. Popular shows include *Sesame Street, Friends, Sex and the City, South Park, The Simpsons, Full House, Gray's Anatomy, American Idol,* and reality shows.

Communications: Smartphones, texting, and social media such as Myspace, Facebook, and Twitter.

Technology: Laptops and tablets.

Popular music: Rap, rock, R&B, pop, Britney Spears, Justin Bieber, Usher, Taylor Swift, LL Cool J, Santana, Christina Aguilera.

Diversity: Celebrate and stretch the meaning of diversity.

Parenting styles: Helicopter parents and parents as friends.

Ethics as people came to adulthood: Figuring out how to balance feelings and doing.

Youth attitude: Rewrite the rules.

If this little snapshot of the generations sparks your interest, I encourage you to research the topic further. It can give you new perspective on how you were influenced by your times—perhaps more than you realized.

Identifying Your Generational Values

What were some of the pivotal national and cultural events that had an effect on how you think about the world? List at least three here. (They need not be items in the lists above.)

_____

_____

_____

What conclusions about yourself and life did you draw from these events or other generational experiences?

_____

_____

_____

How does your place in the stream of history influence your values system? I'll use myself as an example: Having been in high school and college in the mid-to-late 1960s, I was in the thick of the national debate about the Vietnam War, the civil rights movement, and the emergence of feminism. My friends and I were interested in experimenting with new forms of living, such as food co-ops, communes, and crafts-based businesses. Peter, Paul, and Mary and Pete Seeger brought politics into music, singing about social justice and freedom. The impact of those influences on my formative years was considerable. I'm far more interested in social justice than my Silent Generation parents, and also far more willing to question authority. Like many of my peers, I worked on my self-esteem through workshops and therapy. I continue to value social equality, active participation in shaping my world, and self-knowledge. And yes, I still like folk music.

Which of your values do you think come from growing up in your generation?

_____

_____

_____

Self-Esteem Dilemmas

Whatever generation we're in, we continually and gradually develop our values system. However, there are also times that push us to take a leap. They often involve situations where we have to make a moral decision or take a stand. What they have in common is the sense that we must do something if we are to stay true to ourselves and thrive, no matter how difficult the situation may seem.

Consider Mike, who found himself in a painful self-esteem dilemma when he was faced with a troubling ethical choice. As the computer tech at a large private school, he stumbled on the fact that a beloved and effective teacher was using student funds to take her husband along whenever she chaperoned student trips. He knew that calling attention to his discovery would cause a huge upheaval within the school, so he tried to rationalize not speaking up. He thought of the teacher as a good person who was an important positive influence on troubled students. Since the teacher wasn't paid for her time on student trips, he thought to himself, *Maybe it's only fair that her husband goes along.* On the other hand, not reporting his discovery would mean he was supporting what was essentially a theft, even though doing so would maintain the teacher's positive contributions to the school. Mike took pride in seeing himself as a thorough worker. He also took pride in being a compassionate person.

Mike was confronting a classic self-esteem dilemma. He was conflicted because he had to somehow reconcile seemingly conflicting values. What should he do? What would you do? Whatever your reply may be, one thing is clear: values dilemmas like Mike's aren't simple. Mike has to find a way to do what he thinks is right, and do it in a way he can live with (in other words, feel good about). For him, it's not as simple as whether or not to report what he discovered. Because Mike is a compassionate and creative person, hopefully he'll find a solution to his dilemma that somehow reconciles the two sides of the issue—at least enough that he can live with it.

When we're confronted with painful values dilemmas, it's tempting to try to avoid the issue or rationalize a choice that doesn't feel 100 percent okay. Being human, we're bound to give in to these temptations once in a while. If we are to become stronger and grow through those moments, it's essential to remind ourselves that we have a choice. We can seek the help we need to take advantage of the opportunity to grow, or we can sink into inaction, anxiety, or depression. We can stay true to our values, or we can shore ourselves up with excuses.

People who have genuine self-esteem don't like self-esteem dilemmas any more than anyone else. But the combination of their desire to feel good about themselves and their dedication to doing the right thing gets them through. The self-esteem dilemmas they encounter in life only reinforce their personal strength and help them grow.

Identifying Self-Esteem Dilemmas That Have Influenced Your Values

Think of a time when your values were put to the test and you believe you did the right thing, with a positive result.

Briefly describe the situation here:

_____

_____

Which of your values were being challenged at the time?

_____

_____

In hindsight, what impact did the experience have on how you live your life?

_____

_____

_____

_____

However we arrive at it, our system of values provides us with our internal compass for making worthwhile and worthy decisions. Often we don't give our system much thought. We just do what feels right at the time. Our intuitive sense of what's right and good guides our choices and decisions almost automatically. It is only in situations where our values are in conflict with those of others, or where some of our own values and goals seem mutually exclusive, that we have to sit down and carefully figure out what we believe is the right way to manage the dilemma.

Looking at How Your Values Impact Your Life

The following exercise can give you further insight into what makes a decision feel good and right to you. Begin by reading through the list of values words below. Because there are hundreds of words for values, I've limited this list to forty-two of the more common ones. If the list doesn't include values that are important to you, add them in the spaces provided at the end. (For a downloadable version of this exercise, visit http://www.newharbinger.com/31021; see the back of the book for instructions on how to access it.)

____ Achievement	____ Adventure	____ Ambition
____ Beauty	____ Bravery	____ Cheerfulness
____ Closeness	____ Comfort	____ Compassion
____ Competence	____ Cooperation	____ Creativity
____ Fairness	____ Fitness	____ Forgiveness
____ Generosity	____ Growth	____ Health
____ Honesty	____ Humility	____ Imagination
____ Independence	____ Kindness	____ Logical thinking
____ Loyalty	____ Morality	____ Obedience
____ Open-mindedness	____ Passivity	____ Patriotism
____ Play	____ Politeness	____ Power
____ Relaxation	____ Responsibility	____ Self-control
____ Self-reliance	____ Spirituality	____ Usefulness
____ Warmth	____ Wealth	____ Winning
____ Other:_____	____ Other:_____	____ Other:_____

Now read through the list again and do the following:

1. Put a W next to the five qualities that are most important to you in your work. (For the purposes of this exercise, work also includes school, homemaking, and so on.)

2. Put an L next to the five that are most important to you in your love life.

3. Put an F next to the five that are most important to you in friendships.

4. Put an R next to the five that are most important to you in your recreational activities.

Next, identify your top five values, choosing the five that are most important to you. Rank them from 1 to 5 and list them below:

1. _____

2. _____

3. _____

4. _____

5. _____

Now take some time to review your responses to all of the exercises in this chapter. You've gathered a lot of data about your values system. Notice whether there are any patterns. Devote some thought to what you learned about yourself through this process, or what you relearned or affirmed. Then record your observations below. It isn't necessary to complete all three sections below. Just fill in those that are relevant to you.

I learned that I _____

_____

_____

I relearned that I _____

_____

_____

I never realized that I _____

_____

_____

Why does this matter? Because our values are the basis of the "doing good" part of genuine self-esteem. They are what guide our point of view in any decision, conflict, or compromise. When we feel stuck, we can be true to what is most personally important if we are aware of our values and factor them into our thinking.

Let's Review

We are not passive recipients of our values. As we grew up, we continually shaped and refined our values system. We learned it's not such a good idea to take the last cookie or to ask people intrusive questions (even though we'd sometimes like to). Depending on the values of the important people around us, we learned that being honest is good or that we are only required to be honest if someone in authority is looking. We learned that trusting others is a good thing or learned to always be wary of other people.

As our world opened up beyond our household to the neighborhood, school, and larger community, we expanded our personal pool of values teachers and experienced more and more self-esteem dilemmas. We began to think for ourselves. Sometimes we recommitted to the values we had learned. Sometimes we rejected them in favor of other values that we thought would work better for us in our lives. Those self-esteem dilemmas pushed us to think hard about our values and to make choices we could live with. As we grew, we catalogued those conclusions into a personal code of ethics. It's a process that slows down but never stops.

Most of the time, we take our values system for granted. In our day-to-day lives, we automatically make choices based on what feels natural, good, and right. As long as our internal values system is positive and strong, that's fine. But if we need to make a values adjustment in order to be more worthy, exercises like those in this chapter can be helpful in going from wrong to strong. We can make a conscious decision to live a more worthy life.

In his book *The Psychology of Self-Esteem*, Nathaniel Branden says, "No one is coming" (2001, 259). What he means is that we each have to take care of our own self-esteem. Ultimately, we all have to make the choice to aim for a good, just, and moral life and develop the values and commitment that are the basis for such a life. Friends, family, professionals, and books can give us suggestions and support, but in the end it's up to each of us to make a simple yet earthshaking decision: that we are each responsible for how we deal with whatever comes up and how we treat others along the way.

Remember, no one is coming—but you.

CHAPTER 3

Self-Care and Getting Ready for Change

Take care of your body. It's the only place you have to live.

—Jim Rohn

f you want to dive right into learning techniques for increasing your genuine self-esteem, you might be tempted to skip this chapter. But based on my thirty-five years in the mental health business, I've come to appreciate that not all apparent mental health problems are in people's heads—or in their self-esteem. Sometimes there's another issue that needs attention.

I therefore encourage you to read this chapter carefully. After all, the first step in solving any problem is making sure you're addressing the right problem in the first place. If you have a toothache, you don't take stomach medicine to ease the pain. If you're fighting with your lover, you can't fix it by taking a drug. Working on your self-esteem will only pay off if a crisis of self-esteem is really the problem.

Make Sure Self-Esteem Is the Problem

In a classic "which came first, the chicken or the egg" dilemma, people sometimes get caught in an unproductive cycle that goes something like this: *I'm depressed (or anxious). I feel bad about myself for not being able to fix it. That makes me feel more depressed and anxious, which makes me feel even worse—which makes me feel like a pathetic and hopeless human being.* You get the idea: self-esteem gets tied up with feelings of being stuck, upset, or hopeless.

In fact, there are lots of reasons people might feel depressed, anxious, or bad about themselves. The problem may not lie in either their feelings of self-worth or their worthiness as a human being. Their values system may be fine. They may have every reason to feel good about themselves. But they feel bad about themselves because they just plain feel bad and can't find a cause. Therefore, they come to the conclusion that they have a psychological problem. A health care professional may even have told them the problem is "all in your head." Well, not necessarily. Not all symptoms that look psychological are in the head. Sometimes they're in the body. Sometimes they may even be due to what we put in our bodies (food, alcohol, medications, or street drugs) to try to feel better.

Rule Out Medical Issues

There are many medical conditions that can quietly undermine anyone's efforts toward living a worthy and just life. You are one whole person. If your body isn't healthy, your mind and heart can't function as well as they could. Here are just a few of the medical conditions that can look like psychological issues (Kolbasovsky 2008; Morrison 1999).

This medical condition...	...can look like this psychological problem
Alcohol abuse	Depression
Alzheimer's disease	Depression, memory loss, problems with concentration
Anemia (iron deficiency)	Anxiety, depression
Congestive heart failure	Delusions
Constipation	Anxiety, depression, irritability
Diabetes	Depression

Electrolyte imbalance	Delusions, depression
Hormone imbalance	Depression, irritability
Lyme disease	Depression, fatigue
Narcotics addictions	Depression
Poor nutrition	Depression, fatigue
Restless legs syndrome	Depression, fatigue
Sleep apnea	Anxiety, depression, fatigue
Thyroid problems	Anxiety, confusion, delusions, depression, hallucinations, irritability
Urinary tract infection	Anxiety, depression, irritability
Vitamin B_{12} deficiency	Delusions, depression, fatigue

A woman wrote to my advice column asking what to do about her mother, who provided day care for her three young children. Her mother seemed unusually preoccupied and was talking about how she just couldn't live with herself if she didn't find a way to exorcise the devil that sometimes possessed the kids—something not at all in keeping with her mom's usual behavior. *Yikes!* I thought. *This could end very badly.* I immediately thought of news stories about mothers who had drowned their kids because of thoughts like this. "Stop leaving your kids with Grandma *right now*," I wrote, "and take her to her medical doctor for a checkup right away! The doctor should be able to determine if this is a physical or psychiatric problem."

Several months later, she was kind enough to write back. The doctor had diagnosed her mother with a vitamin B_{12} deficiency. After receiving just two vitamin B_{12} shots, her mother stopped thinking that she needed to deal with the devil to do the right thing and feel good about herself. The kids' mother was greatly relieved. So was I.

See Your Doctor

If you suffer from anxiety, fatigue, delusions, depression, or irritability, this may be entirely unrelated to issues of self-esteem. Please see your primary care physician for a complete medical workup to make sure there isn't an underlying medical problem. If you and your doctor don't look for underlying medical problems, you won't find any. Ask for a complete and thorough screening.

If you're told that your problem is all in your head and you're convinced it's not, seek a second opinion. This is serious. If you do have a medical issue and you spend your time and money getting counseling instead of medical help, it will be a waste of time at best. At worst, your health may decline even more. If you have a medical condition, taking antidepressants and spending an hour a week talking about how you aren't getting better simply won't help.

> In 1935, George Gershwin, composer of such works as *Rhapsody in Blue* and *Porgy and Bess*, started experiencing significant depression. He sought out a psychoanalyst, but months of analysis didn't help. A year later he started having blinding headaches and complained that he often smelled something like burning garbage or rubber. Doctors couldn't find a physical cause, so they decided he was probably suffering from "hysteria." Less than a month later, he collapsed into a coma. Only then did doctors discover that he had a brain tumor. Surgery was unsuccessful, and America lost one of its greatest composers at the age of only thirty-eight.

One more thing: If you're sick, that doesn't mean you can't be depressed, anxious, or suffering from another psychological problem. And if you're depressed, anxious, or suffering from another psychological problem, that doesn't mean you can't have a physical illness too. Make sure you and your doctor don't fall into either-or thinking. Our minds and bodies don't live on separate planets. They are interrelated and often affect each other.

Rule Out Medication Side Effects

Medication side effects and interactions can also cause thoughts and feelings that mimic psychiatric symptoms. In addition, side effects of psychiatric medications can actually cause or exacerbate psychological problems. Here are some common side effects of certain classes of medications (Aronson 2008).

These psychiatric medications...	...can cause or intensify these problems
Antianxiety drugs	Aggression, disinhibition
Antidepressants	Agitation, anxiety
Antipsychotics	Depression, fatigue
Mood stabilizers	Problems with concentration and memory
Seizure medications	Fatigue, irritability
Sleep medications	Aggression, confusion, depression, disinhibition, forgetfulness

And that's just for psychiatric drugs! If you're taking any medication, whether for a psychiatric diagnosis or a medical condition, it's important to be aware of potential psychological side effects. Ask your doctor or pharmacist about the potential downsides of any prescribed or over-the-counter medication you're taking.

Sometimes we have to weigh the risks and benefits of medications. If you're depressed, all the self-esteem exercises in the world won't help you feel better about your life if your depression is caused or exacerbated by medication you're taking. But if medication is staving off more serious depression or a serious medical problem, discontinuing it to work on self-esteem could be a mistake. In any case, don't discontinue current medications without consulting with your doctor. Working together, perhaps you can find a way to treat both problems.

Rule Out Effects of Cold Medications, Supplements, and Certain Foods

Over-the-counter medications aren't harmless either. Common cough syrups and over-the-counter cold and flu remedies can interact badly and even dangerously with psychiatric medications. Common active ingredients in these medications that interact poorly with psychiatric medications include pseudoephedrine, diphenhydramine, dextromethorphan, and guaifenesin (Graedon and Graedon 1995). If you're taking prescription medications, it's best to consult with your doctor or pharmacist before heading to the drugstore for something to manage sneezes or coughs.

Please be aware that just because something is "natural" doesn't mean it's harmless. Any ingredient in supplements that has a positive effect on the body or mind also has the potential to have negative effects. For example, a few years ago, the herbal supplement Saint-John's-wort was popular for treating depression. Though it's been found to be effective in treating minor to moderate depression for some people, studies haven't yielded consistent results regarding its helpfulness in treating major depression (Lecrubier et al. 2002). If you quit taking prescription antidepressants, deciding to use Saint-John's-wort instead, and you still feel depressed, your self-esteem may not be the problem. You could be one of the people who needs a prescription antidepressant to get your symptoms under control. Check with your psychiatrist or prescribing professional for advice.

Even a common food can be a culprit. Grapefruit juice is a healthy way to get vitamin C, but the list of medications that react badly to it is very, very long. Grapefruit juice actually boosts the impact of Valium (diazepam), Halcion (triazolam), Versed (midazolam), Buspar (buspirone), Zoloft (sertraline), and Tegretol (carbamazepine) by blocking an enzyme that helps the body absorb them more gradually. This isn't a good thing. Blood levels of these medications can go dangerously high. If you are starting (or taking) medication, be sure to ask your prescriber if there are foods you should avoid.

You're an important member of your medical team. If you feel less than okay, you need to collaborate with your primary care physician and other doctors. Don't expect them to figure out your problems on their own. They need you to do your share by providing information.

Assessing Your Personal Health Habits

Use the form below so you can more easily share key information with your doctors. (For a downloadable version of this form, visit http://www.newharbinger.com/31021; see the back of the book for information on how to access it.) Be honest about your use of caffeine, nicotine, alcohol, or recreational drugs. List any medications or supplements you take, including vitamins, dietary supplements, and over-the-counter medications. Remember, if you have an undiagnosed or undertreated medical condition, or if you're experiencing side effects from prescription medications, street drugs, or interactions among your medications or between foods and medications, all of the self-esteem activities in the world won't fix the problem.

Personal Health Inventory

Number of cups of coffee and caffeinated drinks I have per day: _____

Number of sugared drinks I have per day: _____

Do I drink alcohol? _____ What kind and how much? _____

_____

Do I smoke? _____ How much on average per day? _____

Do I use recreational drugs? _____ What kind and how much? _____

_____

Number of hours of sleep I average each night: _____

Medications I take (list all medications, over-the-counter drugs, vitamins, supplements, and other remedies you take, including dosage and any side effects you've noticed):

_____

_____

_____

_____

_____

_____

_____

_____

If you think nutrition may be part of your problem, keep a diary of everything you eat each day for at least two weeks.

Take Time for Physical Preparation

As tempting as it may be to jump right into working on increasing your genuine self-esteem, you really can't do so without paying at least some attention to your physical self as part of the project. It's often been said that our body is our temple. It is our shelter and source of physical comfort or pain. If you feel lousy in it, it's much more difficult to take on any new project.

Taking care of yourself isn't a block to getting started. It's an important first step. Of course, being healthy does take some work. It means eating right, getting enough sleep, getting away from electronic devices and into the outdoors once in a while, and exercising—hopefully doing something you enjoy, rather than just slaving at a gym, unless you like that kind of thing. It also means being in control of your use of alcohol, recreational drugs, caffeine, and nicotine. Let's take the important elements of self-care one at a time.

Nutrition

Concerns about healthful eating aren't new. As long ago as the fourth and fifth century BC, Hippocrates advocated dietary approaches to treating disease. And yet the need to eat healthy foods seems to go to the bottom of the priorities list for many Americans. In one study, a researcher analyzed information from 4,700 adults who were asked to keep a diary of everything they had eaten in the previous twenty-four hours. Nearly one-third of their calories came from junk food (Block 2004). The result, besides the current obesity epidemic, is that people who eat so much junk food are more vulnerable to medical crises and earlier loss of brain function.

Healthy eating is essential to feeling good about ourselves. Eating right can prevent and control health problems like heart disease, high blood pressure, migraines, and diabetes and can also help us stay sharp as we age.

Breakfast really is the most important meal of the day—for kids and adults. After the "fast" called sleep, the body and the brain need fuel. By recharging your system with breakfast, you'll perform better in just about everything. I teach a university class at 8:30 in the morning. Ugh. Students slouch in, having just rolled out of bed. Some even show up in pajamas! Early every semester, I give a lecture about the importance of eating breakfast to get a kick-start on the day (and give students permission to bring food to class with them). Some of the kids take me seriously. Those who bring, say, yogurt and a piece of fruit to eat at the beginning of class are observably more able to wake up, participate, and do well on quizzes and exams. So eat a healthy breakfast! Doing well in your life is at least as important as getting an A on one of my tests.

Throughout the day, you know what you're supposed to eat: lots of veggies and fruits, whole, unprocessed foods, healthy fats in moderation, and only minimal salt and sugar. Limit packaged and fast foods. Keep the food groups in mind and don't eat too much of anything—even a good thing. If you need help in this area, there are plenty of books, websites, and self-help groups that can give you a boost. If it's a matter of self-discipline, make a promise to yourself to do better. You'll feel better. As an added bonus, you'll probably look better too, which is often a big boost to the old self-esteem!

A final note on diet: Over the last decade, there's been increasing awareness that gluten sensitivity may be a culprit when people feel bad. In addition to causing bloating, stomach-aches, and diarrhea, gluten (found in wheat, rye, barley, and spelt) is also thought to cause increased anxiety or depression, mood swings, and attention deficit disorder (Niederhofer and Pittschieler 2006). A simple way to test for this is to simply do a one- or two-week trial in which you stop eating anything that has gluten in it, such as bread, pasta, cereals, and any other products made from the grains mentioned above. If you notice any appreciable difference in how you feel, talk to your doctor.

Exercise

As with diet, the link between exercise and health has long been acknowledged. Nineteenth-century British politician Edward Stanley once said, "Those who think they have not time for bodily exercise will sooner or later have to find time for illness" (1894, 230). Exercise can improve mood and energy, may reduce stress, and can help you sleep better. Getting physical also causes your brain to release chemicals called endorphins, which may make you feel happier and more relaxed. Regular exercise will keep your brain and judgment sharp as you age. A good, brisk walk at lunchtime will do more for your morale and self-esteem than a trip through the fast-food lane. Doing some kind of workout a few times a week for twenty to thirty minutes will help you feel more virtuous (doing good) as well as more physically fit.

> My son-in-law used to joke that he would only run if he found himself being chased, and even then he would stop to consider if the effort was worth it. His wife, my sometimes slightly sadistic daughter, challenged him to take up running. Because he's the kind of guy who's usually up for a challenge, he decided to go for it. He reported that the first run was brutal, especially since he was outpaced by my daughter, whose running style is more like prancercizing. The second time was easier, and the third time was easier yet. Now, much to his astonishment, most days he laces up his sneakers for a run. He says he feels generally healthier, is more alert throughout his workday, and has energy left over to do things after work, instead of flopping down on the couch.

You know what to do. Now start doing it, even if just a little. Take a walk during your lunch break. Go for a swim a few times a week. Use that stationary bike you bought a few years ago for exercise, instead of as a place to pile clothes. If you have trouble sticking with your commitment to exercise, enlist a buddy to exercise with. You'll both be more likely to stick with it.

Sleep

The average adult needs in the range of six to eight hours of sleep per night in order to be rested. According to data collected between 2005 and 2007, nearly 30 percent of adults got six hours of sleep or less each night (Schoenborn and Adams 2010). That doesn't surprise me. Many adults are so stressed by whatever crises they're experiencing in their lives that they have trouble falling asleep or staying asleep at night. If you're one of them, you may not realize what it's costing you in terms of your mental and physical health.

It isn't clear exactly why the body requires sleep, but we do know that inadequate sleep can have negative effects on health. Sleep is essential for normal immune system function and the ability to fight off disease. It's also crucial for normal nervous system function. If you've ever pulled an all-nighter, whether to study for a test or to care for an infant or a sick child, you know how hard it is to get through the next day. Your mind and body just want to go back to bed!

> Linda didn't believe that sleep had anything to do with her depression. Most nights she worked a late-afternoon to midnight shift, then spent several hours playing an online video game when she got home. She believed she could compensate for staying up until the wee hours of the morning by sleeping late the next day. But I suspected that sleep deprivation was contributing to her depressed mood. I asked her to keep a careful sleep journal for a week, recording when she finally got to sleep, when she woke up, and every time she got up during the night. She was surprised to discover that she was only getting four to five hours of sleep each night and that her sleep was frequently interrupted. She reluctantly agreed to experiment with getting eight hours of continuous shut-eye per night for three weeks. It wasn't at all surprising to me that her depression lifted considerably.

If the reason you aren't getting enough restorative sleep is that you're staying up much of the night to play an online game or chat via Facebook, cut it out! In a recent study, people were given iPads to use during the two hours before bedtime. Their levels of melatonin, the hormone that helps us get to sleep and stay asleep, dropped by 22 percent (Sutherland 2012).

Enjoy your screen time, but finish up a couple of hours before bed so you can get the six to eight hours of sleep you need.

Habits and Addictions

Various lifestyle habits are part of a complete health picture. If you think you can only get through the day with ten cups of coffee, several caffeinated sodas, and a pack of cigarettes, or if you're out of control when it comes to alcohol or recreational drugs, you're doing damage to your body and your self-esteem. You probably beat yourself up regularly about how you should cut down or stop these habits. You may nag yourself about how they divert your time, attention, and money away from your job, friends, partner, or family. You may even feel guilty about indulging in habits that feel good at the time but are ultimately damaging your health. Sorry. Feeling guilty isn't the same as doing something about it. Enough said.

Self-Care Inventory

Even if you're feeling generally healthy, it's a good idea to take a systematic look at your lifestyle and try to identify areas where you could take better care of yourself. Read through the categories in the following worksheet and check off areas where you're doing okay. Then reconsider each category and honestly note whether there's room for improvement. Also note whether it would be a good idea to talk with your doctor before making any changes. (For a downloadable version of this inventory, visit http://www.newharbinger.com/31021; see the back of the book for instructions on how to access it.)

_____ Medical issues: _____

_____

_____

_____ Medication issues: _____

_____

_____

____ Nutrition: _____

_____

_____

____ Exercise: _____

_____

_____

____ Sleep: _____

_____

_____

____ Habits and addictions: _____

_____

_____

Now take another look at what you've written. Think of one small change you could make to improve your self-care and commit to doing it for one week. If you can make even a small change, you'll start to feel better physically and mentally. You'll feel better about yourself. Stick with your changes for at least a month, and you'll feel even better! Once you are successful with making one change, you may be inspired to make others.

Just one word of caution: do cut yourself some slack as you begin making changes. If you're too ambitious you might get discouraged. Start small. Take it in steps. Each step you take will help. Now, with that in mind, write your goal or goals for change over the next week:

_____

_____

_____

_____

Which Comes First: Self-Esteem or Self-Care?

Clients have often said to me, "When I have better self-esteem, I'll take better care of myself." Well, maybe. But it's also possible to run it the other way. If you start valuing your health and well-being enough to take care of yourself, you'll feel better about yourself for doing so, and your genuine self-esteem will grow. You might even find that feeling and looking better improves both parts of your self-esteem (feeling and doing) so much that you don't need the rest of this book!

My son, who's a personal trainer, is convinced of it. He tells me that people who initially come to him to get their bodies in shape are often pleasantly surprised at how much sharper they feel mentally, how much more energy they have, and how much happier they feel in general after they start taking their physical health more seriously.

You may already do a pretty good job of taking care of yourself. Whatever you're doing may be enough, even if, for now, you're letting some self-care choices sit in quadrant 1 (low sense of worthiness and low self-regard). It may be okay to let them go and make peace with them. Maybe you've made a clear decision to not beat yourself up about not losing that last ten pounds, or not giving up your second cup of morning coffee or your one cigarette a day. Or maybe you have to put certain self-care changes on hold while you attend to other issues that are more important to you. That's fine. The important thing is to be honest with yourself and make a conscious choice to be as good to yourself as you can. If you're generally in good shape in terms of health, you can always come back to further improving your self-care later. If you generally live in quadrant 3 (genuine self-esteem), you can afford to leave those last ten pounds in quadrant 1.

Make a Commitment to Making Change

The first step—making a commitment to yourself—might seem like it should be easy, but for many people it can be the most difficult. Somehow it's often much easier to make and keep commitments to other people. We want to please. We don't want to let people down, especially the people who care about us. Each of us wants to be the kind of person who keeps promises to others. But our good intentions often fall apart when it comes to promises we make to ourselves, especially when those promises have to do with self-care. Too often, those promises get put aside for later, after we've taken care of other people or accomplished some task. Somehow, later never comes.

But the truth is this: if we don't take care of ourselves, we can't be very helpful to others. Anyone who's ever gone on an airplane knows the drill. A flight attendant tells passengers that if the air masks come down, they should put on their own mask first, then help others around them. Why? Because you can't help others if you yourself can't breathe. This is a useful metaphor. We can't help others if we're preoccupied with our own suffering.

Given that you're still reading this book, there's a part of you that's contemplating getting ready to make important changes. Give yourself credit for that! Yes, it is possible to reset the self-esteem button. However we were raised, whatever detours away from self-esteem we've taken ourselves on, we remain the creators of our present reality. Once we claim the status of being grown-ups, we can take charge of our own life story.

If you want your life to be better, promise yourself that you'll take the time and make the effort to do what you know you have to do. Now, can you take a deep breath and fill out the commitment contract that follows? You need not use the following form. You can write out your own commitment, phrasing it in whatever way speaks to you. Whatever you choose, take it seriously. Sign it. Look at it every day to help you stay on track.

Hear Ye! Hear Me!

I hereby promise myself that I will work on my genuine self-esteem by spending at least _____ minutes a day learning more about it and practicing activities that enhance self-esteem.

Signed: _____

Date: _____

Let's Review

If we want to live a successful life that's generally satisfying and includes positive relationships, we need to work on both parts of genuine self-esteem: feeling good and doing good. This chapter focused on the feeling good part, recognizing that "feeling good" means being physically healthy as well as having positive emotions.

In fact, the two aren't as separate as American culture sometimes seems to suggest. Personal trainers, nutritionists, and other medical and mental health professionals tell us that people who feel good physically generally feel good mentally and emotionally. We know it too—even when we pretend we don't. We know that when we get enough sleep, eat a healthy diet, get some exercise, and stay away from unhealthy habits and addictions, we are better able to be good to ourselves and others.

Self-care does take work. It doesn't happen by just wishing it were so. It means being a knowledgeable and active member of our own medical team and using but never abusing the recommendations, medications, and treatments available to us when we're ill. It takes time, attention, and, sometimes, willpower. But when we take care of ourselves, we are sharper, clearer, more energetic, and more able to do the things we need and want to do. Feeling good sets us up to do good.

As this chapter drew to a close, I asked you to make a commitment. Now that you understand the two-part model of self-esteem, have explored your own value system, and have reviewed the importance of self-care, you may have a better understanding of why your self-esteem has felt shaky. If you want to feel better about yourself and do better in your life, it's time to take that understanding to the next level: making a commitment to change. The rest of this book will give you tools you can use to follow through on that commitment.

CHAPTER 4

Courage

Life shrinks or expands in proportion to one's courage.

—Anaïs Nin

If you value yourself enough to take care of yourself; if you've ruled out medical and physical issues as the root of your problems; if you're committed to feeling better and doing better in life but you're stuck in quadrants 1, 2, or 4 most of the time—it's time to do something different. Clearly, whatever you've been doing isn't fixing your life. But making change, even positive change, is scary. You may be thinking, *What if I do the wrong thing? What if it's too hard? What if I don't succeed? What if, what if, what if…*

Let's face it: It takes courage to admit that your life isn't working out. It takes courage to try something new and different, especially if it seems out of character to you or to the people around you. It takes courage to put your values into action. This chapter will help you find the courage you need to build or rebuild your genuine self-esteem so that you can live much of your life firmly in quadrant 3.

Putting Values into Action

Having good values to guide your life isn't enough; you have to find the courage to act on them. Having genuine self-esteem requires that we do worthwhile things in order to feel good about ourselves. Yet sometimes people become so discouraged that they're unable to take action. If you relate to any of these comments from my advice column files, you may be feeling as discouraged as these people are:

◊ "Whatever I try to do ends up wrong. Whatever situation I try to handle turns out more messed up. I just feel I'm good for nothing. My friends probably don't care about me. I just keep feeling lonely all the time."—Fifteen-year-old girl

◊ "I got laid off over a year ago. I have a great idea for a new business, but I can't seem to get anyone to believe in it enough to give me the capital to get started. Now I'm sitting at home not making any money and not feeling motivated to do anything. It seems like there's nothing out there for me."—Thirty-two-year-old mother of two

◊ "I got As and Bs in high school, but no matter how hard I study, I've only been getting Cs in college. My father puts me down for it. My mother makes me feel guilty for getting poor grades when they're paying so much money for my education. I haven't left my dorm room in two weeks. I can't focus on assignments or get to the lab. I wanted to do something with chemistry, but I'll never get into grad school. I should probably just drop out."—Nineteen-year-old college sophomore

These people have become immobilized. They are waiting and hoping that someone else will believe in them, build them up, or at least stop putting them down. Meanwhile, the clock is ticking. Another day or week or month goes by, and nothing changes. If you share their feelings, you too may have become so discouraged that you've stopped trying to make things better. It's time to reclaim your courage.

For starters, note that the word "courage" is within the word "discouraged." Psychologist Alfred Adler often said that the only way forward for any of us when we get into that stuck place is to find the courage within ourselves to make changes and take action, even at the risk of repeated mistakes or failures, and regardless of how others may judge us.

Courage isn't an inherited character trait. It isn't something we either have or don't have. It's a willingness to stand up for what we believe in and take risks in order to move forward, even when it's not at all clear what the result will be. Life, after all, doesn't come with a warranty. Adler taught that to be truly alive requires finding the courage to take chances in order to find our place in the world. Further, he emphasized that when we take risks that are grounded in positive values and an interest in the common good, we are unlikely to go wrong.

There's a famous quote by Thomas Edison about his repeated "failure" in trying to invent a lightbulb. With this statement, he illuminates the benefits of taking a risk and learning from the experience: "We sometimes learn a lot from our failures if we have put into the effort the best thought and work we are capable of" (1921, 89). Edison kept going for it, again and again and again—not just to feel good about himself (although I bet he was pretty pleased with himself when he figured it out) but to light up the world. He had the inner courage to keep going in spite of setbacks and dead ends. The story is a classic example of the two-part definition of genuine self-esteem in action. By feeling good enough about himself to keep at it, he succeeded. By accomplishing something that changed our world for the better, he had reason to feel good about himself.

Quite understandably, you may get discouraged now and then. I imagine even Edison had his bad days. But it's what you do with that feeling that determines whether you start sinking into an immobilizing depression or gather up the courage you need to continue becoming all you can be.

Of course, using courage to do things that are irresponsible, foolish, or illegal doesn't count. That kind of "courage" sits firmly in quadrant 4 (self-centered self-esteem). Courage that takes us to genuine self-esteem (quadrant 3) supports positive personal and social goals. It helps us when we need to stretch beyond our comfort level to aim for worthy goals and do the right things to achieve them. It means having the courage to act on positive values when it's important to do so. That may mean resisting the pressure of friends, family members, or authority figures when they're wrong. It may even mean committing to some level of self-sacrifice or being willing to look foolish in other people's eyes when we're convinced we're on the right path. I assure you, there were people who thought Edison was crazy.

Obstacles to Courage

Everyone has moments of discouragement. Often those moments are based in our anxieties and fears. Sometimes we get in our own way by using strategies to avoid our discouragement that only make things worse. Some of the more common examples are described below.

Fear of Making Mistakes

Elbert Hubbard, an American writer and philosopher who lived at the turn of the twentieth century, is credited with saying, "The greatest mistake you can make in life is to be continually fearing you will make one" (1923, 442). It's true. Many of my clients have been so paralyzed by the fear of making a mistake that they've become unable to make any sort of change. Like the people in the letters quoted at the beginning of this chapter, they've given up on trying and given up on themselves. Sadly, unwillingness to confront the possibility of making a mistake is exactly what stands in the way of being successful.

Rudolf Dreikurs, a student of Alfred Adler, once said that "anybody who is fascinated by the possibility of making a mistake is most liable to make one. Preoccupation with the danger of making a mistake leads you smack into it" (1957, 41). Why? Because people who are worried about making a mistake can create a self-fulfilling prophecy. Because they believe they'll fail, it becomes harder and harder not to. Anxiety about the many ways that things can go wrong adds yet another layer to the problem they were originally trying to solve. They feel increasingly discouraged and certain their efforts will result in disaster. Each mistake serves as yet another piece of evidence that they don't have what it takes to master a skill, manage a problem, or fix a relationship. They then deny or compromise their values about the importance of what they want to do. That loss of courage, the apparent inability to stay true to what's right and good for them, is far more damaging than any mistake they might make. As Rudolf Dreikurs often said, "It is less important *what* mistakes we make than *what we do* after we have made them" (1971, 11).

Worrying What Others Think of You

In Shakespeare's play *Hamlet*, Polonius advises his son to avoid bad company and immoderate ways and "to thine own self be true." Although Polonius was a pompous man who never seemed to know when to shut up, even bores can sometimes give good advice. Living well—doing what's right and good—often means not worrying about what others think of us for doing it. It's more important to worry about what we think about our choices than what others might say or think.

Consider this: School-yard bullies can only get away with bullying when the other kids are more concerned about appearing like squealers than about gathering up the courage to do the right thing. People who hurt their families through addictions, anger, and violence often get away with it for years because those who know about it don't have the courage to "intrude." Lots of good ideas fall by the wayside because the inventor or creator is more worried about being thought of as crazy than invested in pursuing a worthwhile goal. Having genuine self-esteem means sticking by our values and standing up for what we believe in, even when others don't approve of our actions or support our ideas.

Measuring Yourself in Comparison to Others

I recently saw a bumper sticker that said, "Why compare yourself with others? No one in the entire world can do a better job of being you than you." I haven't been able to find out who made that concise and accurate comment, but I just had to include it here because it states an important truth: a surefire way to discourage ourselves is by measuring ourselves in comparison to others. There will always be someone who's making more money or getting better grades, someone who's thinner, more artistic, more intelligent, more athletic, more…whatever.

Give it up. In order to learn, we all need to start at the beginning of our own road. No one becomes accomplished at playing guitar if they give up because they aren't able to replicate Eric Clapton's or Slash's guitar riffs after a week or two. No one masters a foreign language, loses twenty pounds, or designs innovative new computer programs if they're constantly measuring themselves against other people who seem to be more gifted in these areas. Personal courage is just that—personal. We need to stick with what's important to us and build on what we've got, not wish we were someone else.

Saving Face by Giving Up

Another way that people discourage themselves is by coming up with face-saving excuses for mistakes and failures. Some compromise their values and give up on their original goal, opting for an easier one. Others avoid the challenge altogether and tell themselves, *Well, I could do it but I don't have time, I have other priorities,* or *I don't really want to do it.* It's tempting and understandable to get discouraged when we can't find a way to master something we really want to accomplish or do what we know is right.

Yes, sometimes we need to adjust our goals. Perhaps we really don't have time to go the distance, or maybe we get new information that changes everything. Sometimes we decide that something isn't worth the effort after all. But when the issue is a drop in courage, we need to find a way to reclaim it. Otherwise we end up even more discouraged.

Eleanor was one of my students a few years ago. A talented and accomplished young woman, she had every reason to believe that she could be accepted into a top-notch graduate program—every reason, that is, except that she was terrified of rejection. As the deadlines for submitting her applications to various schools approached, she found herself procrastinating and losing track of things she needed to do. One week before the deadlines, she was smart enough to come in for a pep talk. After a long and tearful discussion, she was able to see that she was doing a classic face-saving maneuver. If she didn't file on time, she wouldn't have to face the possibility that no school would want her. The problem wasn't that the applications were too long, too demanding, or too time-consuming. She had tied her self-worth so tightly to getting into a top school that she had lost the courage to try. Once she figured that out, she could address the problem directly. By the way, the happy ending to this story is that Eleanor got into three of the eleven schools she applied to.

Making Excuses

Sometimes people cut off their nose to spite their face. Rather than gather up the courage to confront the task, they slide out of it however they can. They tell themselves and others stories that make giving up look rational, preferable, or even self-sacrificing, but deep down they know it's a sham. In the end, they find themselves even more discouraged than they were in the first place.

Substituting Trying for Doing

Some people cover their discouragement with the excuse that they're trying but not succeeding. They put on a display of often useless efforts and dramatic angst to protect their egos and prevent others (and themselves) from judging them harshly. They have the idea that as long as they can protest that they're trying, they don't need to take the real risk required to be successful. To illustrate the pointlessness of trying, one of my teachers used to say, "*Try* to get out of that chair you're sitting in." When the person started to get up, he'd say, "No. I said *try* to get up." When the person started to get up again, he'd say. "No. *Try.*" Obviously, there's no such thing as trying to get up out of a chair. You're either sitting down or getting up.

Matt came to therapy because he couldn't finish his senior thesis. He'd already been at college for an extra semester and was feeling pressure from his folks to finish. In these kinds of situations, I always start with simple suggestions about organizing, scheduling, and prioritizing. Sometimes people just need a little practical help, especially when they've never done a particular task before. For three weeks, Matt sat with his head hanging, telling me how much he was trying.

It was time to shift gears. I asked Matt what would happen if somehow, magically and unaccountably, his efforts got results and he finished his thesis. That brought him up short. He realized that he would then have to leave school, get a job, and get on with adult life. As long as he couldn't make progress on his thesis, he didn't have to face how scared he was. As long as he was "trying," most people in his life didn't fault him for not finishing. The problem wasn't the writing. The problem was his fear that he didn't have what it took to take on the next stage of life. So we shifted our focus and talked about how he could find his inner courage to face life after school. Bolstered by these conversations, Matt was able to complete his thesis, start applying for jobs, and generally look ahead to the future.

Discouragement Assessment

Are you discouraged? Have you lost your willingness to truly, wholeheartedly go for what you want in life and do what is right along the way? Do you have the courage to follow your beliefs about what's good and right? Are you afraid of what other people think? Read through the following list of statements that indicate discouragement and check off any that apply to you.

_____ No matter what I do, it doesn't make any difference to anyone.

_____ I can't stand the idea of making mistakes.

_____ People will just put me down if I stand up for what I believe in.

_____ I freeze up when I think of confronting someone, even when I know I'm right.

_____ I would hate for people to see that I did my best and I'm still not good enough.

_____ I know that I'll never amount to anything.

_____ I'm as afraid of success as I am of failure.

_____ Other people don't believe in me, so I can't believe in myself.

_____ Other people I know are so much better at doing what I want to do that I don't see the point of even trying.

_____ I really wanted to do something that was important to me, but I backed away from it.

_____ It's too scary to stand out by standing up for what I believe in.

_____ Hey! I may not be able to do _____ very well, but at least I do it better than other people.

_____ Disapproval is hard for me to handle.

If you recognize yourself in even a few of those statements, you need a dose of courage. Genuine self-esteem requires action grounded in positive principles. It requires a certain amount of fearlessness to stand up for what we believe to be right. Excuses aren't accepted. "Trying" isn't good enough. We need to develop ways to undo the discouragement and depression that come from times when we didn't feel up to the task, gave up rather than pushing for what was right, or accepted other people's judgments that we were wrong or were making wrong choices. The key is to learn how to en*courage* yourself. That means being "willing and able to take and utilize your inner resources" to take your mistakes in stride and do what the situation requires (Dreikurs 1957, 48). When you increase your courage, you increase your ability to manage life from a position of integrity.

If you didn't check off any of the items or if only some of the items apply to you once in a while, congratulations. You have the courage you need to proceed successfully in life. You can skip the following activities or do them to reinforce a strength you already have.

Activity Choices for Encouraging Your Discouraged Self

The following activities will help you tap into your inner courage as a step toward developing more genuine self-esteem. Courage is an essential factor in an upward spiral. When we act with the courage of our convictions, doing what we feel is right even when others might not agree—and even when our efforts don't work out as we'd hoped they would—we feel good about ourselves. Feeling positively about ourselves helps us dig deeper and act more courageously. Around and around it goes.

You may believe this kind of courage is beyond you. If so, think about the end of the original *Wizard of Oz* movie. Throughout the story, the Cowardly Lion thought he had no courage. Then the wizard pointed out that he'd shown courage all along. What he didn't have was a way to prove it to himself. So the wizard gave him a medal for bravery.

You've already shown lots of courage in your life. All children are born with it. As you grew and developed your understanding of right and wrong, you learned that doing the right thing got you closer to people and felt better than doing the wrong thing. Growth, moving forward, figuring out how to be fair and share and care, learning to connect positively with others, going where we haven't been before—all are as natural as breathing unless we've become discouraged. As a child, you were no different than any other little kid. Give the following activities a try. They can help your reclaim the courage that is your birthright.

Give Yourself Credit for the Courage You Have

Just like the Cowardly Lion, you too have been courageous in your past. You just don't give yourself enough credit. Remind yourself of some of the times when you've done or said things that required some courage. They don't have to be on the level of saving a life or taking on a mob. Most of our courageous acts are much smaller, quieter things.

Go back as far in time as you need to in order to find a situation where you did the right thing in spite of someone else's opinion, stood up for something you believed in, or persevered in your convictions despite setbacks or mistakes.

Write a description of the situation and what you did:

_____

_____

_____

What made it possible for you to draw upon your courage?

_____

_____

_____

Courage isn't just a feeling; it's an *action*. You made that situation possible. It wasn't fate. It wasn't an accident. You *did* something. You probably did something that improved your life, made someone else's life better, or made a contribution to the world—three things that are often inter-related. It's important to notice your own power and learn from times when you used it for good. Those times are the basis for building the confidence you need to do so again.

Repeat this exercise, this time focusing on a time when you did the right thing even though it was at some cost to yourself. The Cowardly Lion in *The Wizard of Oz* was a wonderful friend to his companions in spite of his belief that he didn't have what it took to deal with stress or confront danger. You've done it too. Reminding yourself of times when you've stood up for others, been a good friend, or supported someone you love even though it was stressful provides object lessons to hold on to when discouragement starts to slide into your thinking.

Write a description of the situation and what you did:

_____

_____

_____

_____

What made it possible for you to draw upon your courage?

_____

_____

_____

_____

The memories you've described here can be touchstones for you. Whenever you have the sinking feeling that you don't have what it takes to stand up and do the right thing, take your mind back to those times. Sit with the memories. Feel them deeply. Then bring those feelings to bear on the current problem. You may find that doing so gives you just the boost of courage you need to try again.

Write a New Script

If you're unconvinced that you've ever done anything that took some courage, make something up. Think about a time when you could have done something better or differently and rewrite the story with a different ending. Many of us are what a friend of mine calls "overnight responders." We think of the perfect thing to say or do once we've had time to think about it. We'd like to be quicker with a retort or action, but we haven't mastered the trick of always doing something the very moment it's called for. That's okay so long as we learn from it.

Choose a situation that's especially troubling to you. Maybe you freeze when you know your opinion differs from those of the people around you. Maybe you find it hard to confront someone who's making a racist or sexist joke or who is otherwise offensive. Unless you rehearse new ways to deal with it, it's likely to happen again.

Now write a script for what you'll do and say next time. Practice it in your imagination. Practice it out loud in the privacy of your home. Practice it until it feels natural. Your problem probably isn't in knowing what you want to say. It's in finding the courage to say it. Practice will make it come more quickly and assertively. (For a downloadable version of this exercise, visit http://www .newharbinger.com/31021.)

My New Script

Situation where I freeze:

_____

_____

What I'll do and say that's different:

_____

_____

_____

_____

_____

With practice, you'll be ready for your next opportunity to handle the situation better.

Learn How to Learn from Mistakes

Fear of making mistakes is a major impediment to doing good. To reclaim your courage, stop hitting yourself on the head with self-blame. Instead, gain some experience with failure to prove to yourself that mistakes aren't the worst thing in the world. Most of the time, they're merely a setback. But even when a mistake creates an uncomfortable situation, there are things to learn from it. Like Thomas Edison, we can only learn by seeing the results of what we do, not by focusing on our good intentions. (For a downloadable version of this exercise, visit http://www.newharbinger.com/31021.)

Think of a time when you "failed" to do the right thing or made a mistake in an interaction with someone else. Set aside your feelings of guilt, shame, disappointment, and self-judgment and describe the situation. Just write down the facts:

_____

_____

_____

_____

Find at least four positive things you learned from it, no matter how small or seemingly insignificant:

1. _____

2. _____

3. _____

4. _____

We can choose to focus on a mistake or a failure of courage, or we can choose to focus on what we've learned. By focusing on learning instead of the mistake, we can keep ourselves engaged with the problem. It's one of the best ways to battle depression and self-blame, which can be so paralyzing.

Repeat this exercise. Repeat it as often as necessary to get yourself back into the mind-set that there are always things to learn from mistakes.

Practice Making Mistakes

Believe it or not, sometimes doing what we fear is exactly what we need to do to conquer the fear. When we decide to do something anxiety-provoking on purpose, we take control of it. By starting small and working up to facing what frightens us, we can gradually master it.

Think of something small you've been hesitant to take on. Maybe it's asserting a difference of opinion with your partner. Maybe it's asking a question in class or at work that others might think is stupid. Or perhaps it's the fear of serving the wrong thing for dinner when a critical and meat-eating relative visits. You get the idea. Describe it here:

_____

_____

_____

Now do it badly. That's right: make a mistake on purpose. Assert a silly opinion about a movie your partner thinks is the best film ever made. Ask a stupid question in class. Serve a tofu stir-fry "by mistake" to someone who only likes his meals bleeding (but do have a backup dish if you think it might spark World War III). It's important to experience that you won't die (or wish you had) if you seem to make a fool of yourself or do something unpopular once in a while. Give yourself some experience with managing embarrassment and the judgments of others. Make a game of it. Come up with funny comments, graceful apologies, and rehearsed comebacks for others' possible negative reactions. ("Oops! Silly me. I forgot the beef stew in the slow cooker.") Intentionally make at least one mistake a day until doing so loses its sting. Keep a little diary of your mistakes below. Or, for a downloadable form, visit http://www.newharbinger.com/31021; see the back of the book for instructions on how to access it.

Date: _____

A mistake I made on purpose: _____

_____

Was it the end of the world? _____

What I learned: _____

_____

Date: _____

A mistake I made on purpose: _____

_____

Was it the end of the world? _____

What I learned: _____

_____

Date: _____

A mistake I made on purpose: _____

_____

Was it the end of the world? _____

What I learned: _____

_____

Repeat this exercise. Repeat it as often as necessary to convince yourself that failing at things doesn't make you a failure. It only helps you grow.

Call In Reinforcements

There's no rule that courage means having to face our fears alone. Often, what we need most is for someone to literally (or verbally) hold our hand. There's no shame in that. Providing mutual support is part of what being fully human is about. It's what good friends and supportive family members do for each other. Think of at least two people you can call on when you need an injection of courage. If you don't have supportive family members or that kind of friend, think of professionals, such as a clergyperson, doctor, therapist, or hotline, you can call to help you find the courage to act. Also set a goal to expand this list. (See chapter 7, on relationships, for some tips on how to do this.)

List people who might provide support here, along with their phone numbers and e-mail addresses:

1. _____

2. _____

3. _____

4. _____

Act "As If"

In his blog at the Huffington Post, Mike Robbins, a motivational speaker, wrote, "If we act 'as if' we already have something we want, act 'as if' something is already occurring in our lives (even if it's not), or act 'as if' we know how to do something (even if we don't)—we create the conditions for it to manifest in our life with greater ease and probability" (2010).

Robbins must have been reading Alfred Adler. Adler thought that most of us act as if our mistaken ideas about ourselves and life are true, when they're actually our own creation (Adler 1964). Since we created those perceptions, we can also create others. Using this idea, Adler developed the "acting as if" technique. He encouraged his clients to begin acting as if they were already the people they would like to be, doing the things they believed they should but for whatever reason felt they couldn't. Acting "as if" lets us try alternative ways of handling situations and operating in the world. It also lowers our risk of feeling foolish or making a mistake, since we can always tell ourselves we're only acting.

Alcoholics Anonymous uses a version of this technique in their saying "Fake it 'til you make it." There is wisdom in this. Sometimes a way to make a personal change is to pretend that we've already done it. With enough practice, it starts to feel natural.

A helpful way to start is to model your behavior after someone else's. Think of someone you know who lives with more genuine self-esteem than you do. In the privacy of your own home, experiment with sitting and standing the way that person does. Think about the energy that person puts out to others. How does he or she do that? Is it the way the person holds his or her head? Is it an expression or tone of voice? Is it an approach to problems? Stand in front of a full-length mirror. Look at yourself and pretend you are that person. See how well you can mimic how that person presents himself or herself.

Now think of a problem you're trying to solve or a challenge you want to meet. How would that person handle it? Role-play that person. Keep looking in the mirror. Do your best to copy how that person would respond. It may feel a bit silly. But get into it. Work on being as true to the person as you can be.

How did that feel? Are there parts of the experience you want to take into a real situation? What did you learn about taking a risk? What are you willing to do differently because of it?

_____

_____

_____

_____

_____

If you decide you want to apply what you've learned and really own it, you need to make a commitment to practice it until it feels more like you.

My client Pearl, a junior in high school, didn't feel as pretty as her name. In fact, she thought of herself as unattractive and clumsy. At sixteen, feeling unattractive is one of the worst feelings there is. She was sure other girls were laughing at her and that she would never have a boyfriend. Her mom's reassurances did no good. I knew better than to try to talk her out of her belief, even though she was a lovely girl. Instead, I asked her to try the "as if" game. (We had enough of a relationship by then for her to humor me.) I asked her to name the girl at school she thought was attractive enough to have whatever friends she wanted. I then took her through the steps outlined above. "Show me how that girl stands, sits, and walks," I said. "How does she react to others?" Pearl stood taller. She walked with more confidence. She looked me in the eye. And as she responded, we talked about how it felt. Then I asked if she could practice the same thing at home. Once she felt she knew the role, could she try it out at school? She said that she really had nothing to lose, so she was willing to try "acting as if" as much as possible over the next few weeks. It wasn't an overnight success. (Few things are.) But over those few weeks, people started to respond to her differently. Because she was more approachable, she started being approached.

Make What Goes Around Come Around

Feeling more courage won't increase your genuine self-esteem unless you do something with that courage. Remember, genuine self-esteem is an interaction of feeling good about yourself and doing things that are worthwhile, commendable, and helpful. So let's get doing!

We can all increase the number of times we act courageously in life. There are lots of small things that might require you to gather up your courage and go a bit out of your way to make a difference. Standing up for someone, expressing an unpopular but valid opinion in class or at a staff meeting, or even taking a spider out of the house because you know someone else is more afraid of spiders than you are—all are expressions of the courage that can empower genuine self-esteem. Of course, larger acts, like organizing a charitable event or writing a letter to the editor to publicly express your opinion about a controversial issue, also increase genuine self-esteem and contribute to making the world a better place. But for now, simply make a commitment to be more courageous in small ways. It will really pay off—for you and for others.

Think of a few small things you could do that take a little more courage than you've been showing. List them here. Make a commitment to do at least one a day.

1. _____

2. _____

3. _____

4. _____

5. _____

If you're ready to take on bigger challenges, that's great! There are so many ways to make a difference by exercising some courage. (I'll outline a few in the pages that follow.) Put yourself out there to be counted.

Get Physical

Many charities hold weekend events that count on people to get active as a way to say, "Yes, this is important enough for me to give of my time and money." Walk for breast cancer. Run for the Special Olympics. Ride for AIDS research. Swim laps for the local high school fund-raiser. Those who participate make an important financial contribution to organizations dedicated to funding research or improving life for people who can't advocate for themselves. Just as importantly, your presence and participation show decision makers in the government or funding institutions that the cause is important to you. If you're not athletic, that's okay. You can always pass out water, check people in or out, staff a food stand, or otherwise provide support. Having the courage to be visibly involved will provide a big boost to your genuine self-esteem. Make a commitment to participate in at least two of these events per year.

This year I will:

1. _____

2. _____

Take a Stand by Standing Up

Every Sunday, there's a vigil on the common in the center of my small town. People stand quietly along the main street holding a banner that says, "War Is Not the Answer." Some of the people have been out there most weeks since the mid-1960s, when they were protesting the Vietnam War. Some are newly there due to concerns about US involvement in the Middle East and Afghanistan. Whether or not passersby agree with their politics, they can't help but be impressed that twenty or more people are out there every Sunday, rain or shine, snow or heat, quietly stating their political view by literally taking a stand.

Similarly, activists are often standing, clipboard in hand, outside local stores, asking those who are interested to sign a petition about some environmental, political, or charitable cause. They too are taking a stand putting themselves out there to collect signatures in support of something they believe in.

These are examples of ways in which people take a stand by literally standing up for what they believe in. It takes courage. Not everyone agrees with them. Sometimes people aren't kind. But they continue to show up. Their efforts often make a difference. Think about ways you can literally take a stand. Can you commit to doing at least one?

I will take a stand by _____

On this date: _____

Take a Stand by Writing

Too shy to put your body on the line? You can still exercise your courage. Writing a letter to the editor of your local newspaper may be an old-fashioned idea, but people still do it to express an opinion, request support for an issue, or thank people who helped make a difference. Social media offers yet more opportunities to take a stand, whether by posting something on your Facebook page, commenting on someone else's post, tweeting, or starting and maintaining a blog. Anything you can do that requires summoning a bit of personal courage to state your convictions will help your genuine self-esteem grow.

Think of a few ways you could build your courage by putting your pen (or keyboard) to the task. List them here and commit to following through on at least one:

1. _____

2. _____

3. _____

Tyler grew up in a family where it was against the rules to talk about anything political. His family hated conflict and therefore discouraged airing conflicting opinions. As a result, Tyler grew up fearful of stating his point of view about anything. That wasn't working for him at all as an economics major at the local university. Professors expected lively debate! The problem wasn't that Tyler didn't have opinions; it was that he needed a big dose of courage to express them. We talked about small ways he could start practicing taking a stand. The local elections were a perfect jumping-off point. He really liked the views of one candidate in particular, so he signed up to work in her campaign headquarters. Just being there helped him feel better. Connecting with people who had strong opinions and welcomed debate helped him let go of his fears.

Remember What This Is All About

Remember, genuine self-esteem has two parts that reinforce and support each other. To live comfortably in quadrant 3, we need to feel good about ourselves and we need to have the courage to do the things that earn the right to feel that way. That's why courage is so central: if we don't have enough courage, we shrink from doing and saying the things we believe are right. That damages our self-esteem.

On the other hand, practicing being courageous, even in small ways, helps us develop our courage muscle for times when we need it. Practice doesn't necessarily make perfect, but it sure does make us feel more ready and confident.

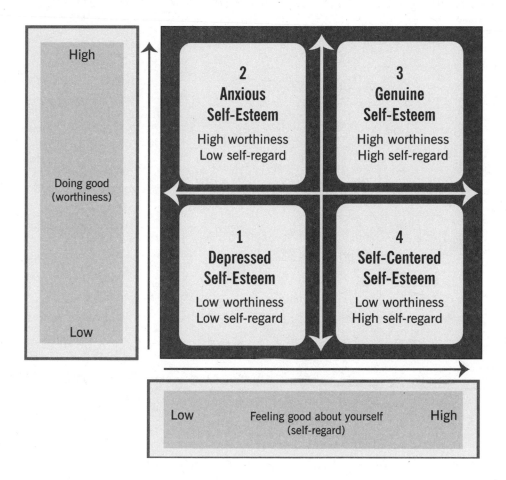

CHAPTER 5

Positivity

Positivity opens us. The first core truth about positive emotions is that they open our hearts and our minds, making us more receptive and more creative.

—Barbara Fredrickson

Negativity has enormous power in our lives. When we focus on the negative, we reinforce our discouragement and drag ourselves down. We get so discouraged that we become immobilized and can't act for our own benefit or the benefit of others. This diminishes our genuine self-esteem. The antidote to this is positivity. This chapter is dedicated to bringing you up to speed on what has been discovered about positivity and how to use it to enhance your genuine self-esteem.

My strongest lesson in positivity came from my grandmother, who lived with me and my family from the time she was eighty-four until her death at age ninety-three. She was a role model for genuine self-esteem for all of us. She spent every morning reading in three things: the daily newspaper, the Bible, and *The Power of Positive Thinking*. When I asked why, she said, "I don't want to be one of those old folks who don't know what's going on. The Bible keeps me connected to God. And that man Norman Vincent Peale knew what he was talking about. You get as good as you do!" That made sense to me.

My grandmother always found a silver lining in every situation. She had nothing but kind words to say to everyone. As bedtime, she thanked those around her for the little things they had done for her that day and thanked God for the blessings in her life. She was truly the most serene and gracious person I've ever met. Little did I know at the time that she was practicing positive psychology well before it was even given a name. She died peacefully in 1989, grateful to the end for the life she felt she'd been given. Of course, in reality it was a life she'd made.

Positive Psychology

Ten years after I had that conversation with Grandma, Martin Seligman, the newly elected president of the American Psychological Association, announced a new direction for psychology. In an interview around that time, he said, "I believe psychology has done very well in working out how to understand and treat disease. But I think that is literally half-baked. If all you do is work to fix problems, to alleviate suffering, then by definition you are working to get people to zero, to neutral. What I'm saying is, 'Why not try to get them to plus-two or plus-three?'" (2002b).

Seligman's work echoes that of Abraham Maslow, who used the term "positive psychology" as early as 1954. He said that a self-actualized person is someone who focuses on his or her talents and strengths. He studied healthy, exemplary people to develop his theories and wrote that "the study of crippled, stunted, immature, and unhealthy specimens can yield only a cripple psychology and a cripple philosophy" (May, Rogers, and Maslow 1984, 171). Although many might find his language pejorative, positive psychologists would argue that he had a point. To understand how to help people overcome illness, we need to study those who are well.

Shifting the Focus from Wrong to Strong

Seligman challenged psychologists to move from thinking about wrong to strong, building on what's already right and good in people, rather than focusing solely on what is weak and sick. Why? Because when people are more negative than not, they don't feel very good about themselves and don't like the rest of us much either. They often don't have the energy or the courage to assert the good and positive that's already in their lives, much less build on it. Yes, psychologists can help people change negative thinking and feel a bit better, but that doesn't necessarily help them get to the flip side: feeling good and doing well. Seligman wanted people to flourish—to get the most out of life, not just to cope. I love that word, "flourish." It means more than just being happy; it means growing and thriving. Seligman embraced the two-part definition of self-esteem, stating, "The feeling of self-esteem is a byproduct of doing well" (2007, 33).

Unlike happiness, which is only an internal feeling state, Seligman emphasizes what he calls "well-being," stating that "well-being cannot exist just in your own head: well-being is a combination of feeling good as well as actually having meaning, good relationships, and accomplishment" (2011, 25).

He summarizes the pillars of positive psychology in the acronym PERMA (2011, 16):

Positive emotion: feeling happy and satisfied with life

Engagement: feeling focused and absorbed in what we do

Relationships: connecting with others; loving and being loved

Meaning: serving something we believe is bigger than the self

Achievement: accomplishing things for their own sake, for the sake of personal growth, and to contribute to the world

Notice that only the first two pillars are about feeling good. The other three are about doing. Seligman makes the point that we can be happy and engaged (feel good) and still be wrong, even deluded. Flourishing requires an interaction among all five elements.

Seligman often quotes the work of Mihaly Csikszentmihalyi, who, in 1990, wrote a groundbreaking book that nudged the contemporary field of psychology toward positivity. Csikszentmihalyi gave a name to one of the best of human experiences: *flow*. "A person in flow," he said, "is completely focused....Self-consciousness disappears, yet one feels stronger than usual. The sense of time is distorted; hours seem to pass by in minutes....In the harmonious focusing of physical and psychic energy, life finally comes into its own" (1997, 31–32).

Artists, craftspeople, and scientists achieve flow when they are totally into whatever they're doing. The rest of us can experience this too, whether doing something as simple as sharing a perfect s'more at a summer campfire or as complicated as designing new software that makes it easier for people to access the Internet. When we aren't invested in being better than others but only in doing our best, we push ourselves to new levels, feel terrific, and make the world a better place. When we're in flow, we aren't anxious, bored, or depressed. When we're in flow, we feel acutely alive.

Notice that flow is about feeling good through doing something good. I hope you've been there at least once. Flow is intoxicating stuff. It happens when we're thoroughly engaged. It's an experience that lies firmly in quadrant 3, genuine self-esteem.

Character Strengths

Martin Seligman found that helping people get in touch with their strengths is what puts PERMA into action. He has defined twenty-four strengths, a word that he uses for "values" (Peterson and Seligman 2004). Each of us has some strengths that are stronger than others. By identifying and using our top strengths regularly, we can be in flow more often and experience a high level of genuine self-esteem (Seligman 2002a). What a wonderful discovery! By building on these strengths—values that we already know to be strong—we can become even stronger and more satisfied with life. This may seem obvious. But all too often we're so focused on improving what we think is wrong with us that we forget that the big payoff comes by starting with what's right. (Stay tuned for an activity later in this chapter that will help you get in touch with your own character strengths.)

Positive psychology asks us to work on—what else?—our positivity. Don't worry; it isn't about unicorns and rainbows. It's not a move to re-create the human potential movement of the 1970s with all its wackiness. It's a new look at what we can do to bring out the best in ourselves and others and the positive effects that doing so has on our lives. Seligman and others in the field of positive psychology aren't just theorists. They've also researched and written about practical ways to tap into our strengths to promote well-being. My grandmother would have approved.

Flourishing, not Languishing

Barbara Fredrickson is one of the top researchers in positivity. She and her colleagues and students have identified that positivity is what can make Csikszentmihalyi's flow happen (Fredrickson 2009). She maintains that positive emotions not only feel good but also widen our possibilities for doing good for ourselves and others. They are what make the difference between flourishing and what she calls languishing. Like Seligman, she says that flourishing is beyond feeling good. It's also about doing good, meaning adding value to the world: "It simply requires transcending self-interest enough to share and celebrate goodness in others and in the natural world" (2009, 17). Sound familiar? She and her team are providing scientific proof that the two-part definition of self-esteem is what we need to understand if we are to live fuller, more satisfying lives.

Fredrickson's most important contribution thus far is probably her discovery that positivity not only cancels out negativity but also helps people *broaden and build* their resources. She found that positive emotions "*broaden* people's ideas about possible actions, opening our awareness to a wider range of thoughts and actions than is typical" (2009, 21). Further, positive emotions *build* our resources for the future by connecting us to others and increasing our sense that we have options for solving problems. "By opening our hearts and minds," she says, "positive emotions allow us to discover and build new skills, new ties, new knowledge, and new ways of being" (2009, 24). In short, positivity contributes to both the feeling good and doing good parts of genuine self-esteem.

The Three-to-One Positivity Ratio

Okay! But how much positivity in our lives is enough? Another of Barbara Fredrickson's significant contributions to positive psychology is her discovery that positivity has a tipping point. Her research shows that people who experience positive emotions versus negative emotions at or above a ratio of three to one flourish. Those who are below a three-to-one ratio languish.

When we succeed at developing a life in which positive experiences that are genuine and sincere outweigh the negative by a ratio of somewhere around three to one (or greater), we set in motion an upward spiral of positive feelings and accomplishments. We become more optimistic and resilient, and we enjoy better connections with others. In short, we flourish.

Note those two important words: "genuine" and "sincere." Simply increasing the quantity of positive statements we make or upbeat moments in our lives isn't enough to put us on an upward spiral. We also have to increase the quality of those experiences. (This corresponds to the principles of Seligman's PERMA.) On the other hand, when we fall below that ratio and the negative outweighs the positive, we set a downward spiral in motion that leads to depression, boredom, and feeling stuck.

An important study that supports Fredrickson's broaden and build theory was conducted by psychologist Sonja Lyubomirsky and her colleagues. They examined almost three hundred studies of positivity (representing more than 275,000 people) that measured people's success in marriage, health, work life, and so on. Regardless of what kind of success was being measured, they found that positivity *produces* success in life as much as it reflects success in life (Lyubomirsky 2008). Think about it. That's a positive, upward spiral. Together, positive feelings and positive actions (the two parts of genuine self-esteem) make us more successful, which makes it more likely that we'll feel positive, and around it goes. Positivity broadens and builds people's capacity to do good and feel great!

Obstacles to Positivity

There are many ideas and attitudes that get in the way of feeling positive and going for that three-to-one positivity ratio. Below, I'll discuss some of the most common obstacles.

Being Wired That Way

For millions of years, human survival depended on knowing what was wrong. For cave people the world was a dangerous place. They were constantly on the alert for saber-toothed tigers and lightning storms. Hypervigilance—being always on the alert for attack or disaster—helped them see what was coming so they could protect themselves and their clan. Getting out of the caves didn't get that sensitivity out of us. Despite the fact that most of us don't face those kinds of immediate threats on a daily basis, our nervous systems can still be easily activated.

Of course, some people do still live in situations where it makes sense to be a little bit paranoid (or even a lot fearful) when walking down certain streets or when certain people come around. Some people have had such traumatic or violent experiences in their home lives, relationships, or wartime situations that they've developed post-traumatic stress disorder (PTSD). Their fight-or-flight response to perceived threats can be triggered very quickly by a particular smell, sound, or sight. PTSD is essentially vigilance on steroids.

This kind of hypervigilance makes sense when survival is at stake. Unfortunately for many people, once their anxiety has been heightened to such an extent, they can't turn it off—even when they are safe, loved, and protected; even when life is going their way. That's where therapy comes in. With the support and guidance offered by therapy, we have the power to rewire ourselves so that old hurts and fears don't continue to dominate our lives.

> Carla was sexually abused by her uncle when she was very young. Funny and playful, he had always acted like her best friend. Then the abuse started. Fortunately, her mother stopped it as soon as she figured out what was going on. But even so, damage had been done. As an adult, Carla became tense and anxious whenever she started to get close to a man. At twenty-five, she came to me for therapy because she had started dating a man who she knew had no intention of hurting her. Nevertheless, she couldn't relax around him. She wondered whether the experience with her uncle was always going to get in the way of relationships. I assured her that it didn't have to. With treatment that focused on her strengths and mindful relaxation, Carla was able to separate her present from her past so she could love and be loved without fear.

Having a Negative Bias

Negativity bias is the psychological term for the very human tendency to remember negative experiences over positive ones. When a kid gets four As and a B, it's almost impossible for the kid or the kid's parents not to wonder, *What's with the B?* If we get a job performance review that scores us high on nine items but suggests we need improvement on a tenth item, where do we go? Straight to that tenth item. We worry and obsess about it. It's an unusual person indeed who thinks, *Wow, I'm 90 percent wonderful!*

Blaming and Shaming

Blaming and shaming are common tools for avoiding personal responsibility and appearing superior to others. Almost everyone has had the experience of being thrown under the bus at one time or another because someone else was avoiding blame. If you feel like you may still have some tread marks on your back, it can be difficult to take initiative or function fully. In some organizations and some families, blame and shame are tossed from person to person in an effort not to be the one blamed or shamed. No one wants to get back under that bus! The only way to avoid it seems to be either to lay low or to establish that other people are guiltier or more wrong. This is a painful way to live. It creates a certain level of paranoia in a group and blocks people from taking healthy risks to solve problems. It certainly squelches creativity and generosity.

Blamers and shamers know, on some level, that they're looking good only at others' expense (an example of living in quadrant 4, self-centered self-esteem). Ultimately, this does as much damage to their self-esteem as it does to the self-esteem of the person they blamed or shamed.

Ruminating

Ruminating means chewing on something mentally. We can drive ourselves ever deeper into negativity by going over and over and over the things we think are wrong, by thinking about all the ways we are to blame, and by repeatedly telling ourselves that we should be ashamed. Not surprisingly, revisiting all of the ways we think we're inadequate, stupid, or bad tends to drive us into depression and make us feel more and more helpless and hopeless.

> Summer is typical of people who are chronically depressed. She grew up in a family where people were hard on her, it's true. But she's even harder on herself. She's convinced she is stupid, ugly, incapable—you name it. She regularly tells herself that she's a hopeless case, that she can't possibly get better, and that she probably deserves to feel the way she feels. She's so depressed that she's defeated several therapists who have tried to help her. She figures that anyone who sees good in her doesn't understand the situation. It will take very gentle and skillful work to help her get her internal critic to shut up and to start rebuilding her ability to see the good in herself.

Thinking It's Un-American

Barbara Fredrickson (2009) has suggested that some people see being positive as un-American. She points to the early influence of Calvinism, a theology that taught it was sinful to enjoy oneself. Instead, one measured people's worth by their hard work and thrift. All in all, it was a rather dour approach to life. The Pil-grims were indeed a grim lot. In fairness, their lives were extremely hard. However, I can't help but think that their lives would have been eased somewhat if they'd allowed themselves to sing out loud and whoop it up a little.

Even though we are now centuries removed from those early Pilgrims, American culture continues to value hard work over pleasure and competition over community. We work more days and longer hours than any other developed country. Yet we're ambivalent about our values in this area. On the one hand, we see kids who do nothing but study as type A over-achievers, but on the other hand we disapprove of kids who don't always try to do their best. We admire hard workers who put in long hours but also criticize them (especially if they're female) if they don't make time to play with their kids. We tend to do and do and do without thinking about whether we're doing good for ourselves and others.

Fredrickson (2009) believes we need to make a fundamental shift and stop seeing doing productive work (doing good) and taking time for pleasure (feeling good) as opposite. In her view, positivity is a means to a better end, rather than an end in itself.

Learned Helplessness

In the early 1960s, Martin Seligman and Steven Maier made an important discovery. In experiments where dogs were repeatedly subjected to shocks they couldn't avoid, the dogs eventually gave up, even when conditions changed and escape was possible. They termed this *learned helplessness* (Seligman and Maier 1967). The same thing can be seen in people. If people feel that they have no control over a situation that's toxic to them or even dangerous, they may give up on trying to get out of it. This is why some women stay in abusive relation-ships. It's why some hostages don't try to escape. It's why people don't report a harassing boss or supervisor. If their past efforts failed repeatedly or made things worse, they may stop trying. Just as a stone can get worn away by drops of water, genuine self-esteem can be worn away when, no matter what someone does to get out of a situation, it does no good. Positivity and mindfulness (the topic of the next chapter) are the antidotes to this.

Positivity Self-Assessment

This exercise will help you assess your current level of positivity. Put an X where you believe you are on each of the scales below. An X in the middle would mean that you're either half and half or neutral.

Optimistic	Pessimistic
Mostly happy	Mostly unhappy
Very self-accepting	Very self-critical
Generous	Selfish
Grateful	Ungrateful
Highly tolerant of differences in people	Highly intolerant of differences in people
Having high standards of right and wrong	Having low standards of right and wrong
Having strong connections with others	Feeling isolated from others
Feeling that your life is meaningful	Feeling that life has no meaning

The more items for which your X is left of the midpoint, the more positivity you already have in your life. No one (or at least no one I know) is all the way to the left on all of them. A reasonable goal is to gradually move your set point to the left on the items where you are most to the right.

Yes, that is possible. Yes, you can be happier and more positive. Researcher Sonja Lyubomirsky (2008) found that only 50 percent of our happiness is genetic (the temperament we're born with), while 10 percent is attributed to life circumstances (such as health, financial situation, or marital status). The other 40 percent is up to us! Therefore, we can deliberately and actively choose or create 40 percent of what makes us happy and in that way, increase our genuine self-esteem. Another researcher, Angela Duckworth, found that "grit" (meaning perseverance and passion for long-term goals) is more important than talent or level of intelligence for achieving our goals (Duckworth et al. 2007). And Alfred Adler was clear that "to live means to develop oneself" (1964, 269). By making a commitment to integrating activities like those in this book into your life, you can increase your sense of self-worth and worthiness and enjoy more genuine self-esteem.

Activity Choices for Adding Positivity to Your Life

For the activities in this chapter, it would be helpful for you to have a small notebook. You can get started without it, but you really need to keep a journal of some kind since most of these activities require making lists and recording insights over several weeks. By doing so, you'll accumulate some data that will be helpful to review every now and then. You'll also have a log of positivity that can provide a morale booster when you need one. Overall, the goal is to increase your positivity ratio to at least three to one to help you build and enhance your genuine self-esteem.

Identify Your Character Strengths

Psychologist Martin Seligman developed a list of character strengths that are found to varying degrees in all of us and that help us flourish (Peterson and Seligman 2004). He sometimes uses "virtues" as a synonym for strengths. As you read the list, it will become apparent he is talking about values. It's a difference of vocabulary but not meaning. His twenty-four character strengths are clustered into six categories:

Wisdom and knowledge

> Creativity
>
> Judgment
>
> Curiosity
>
> Love of learning
>
> Perspective

Courage to meet difficult challenges

> Bravery
>
> Perseverance
>
> Integrity
>
> Enthusiasm

Love and connectedness

> Intimacy
>
> Kindness
>
> Sociability

Participation in community and justice

> Responsibility
>
> Fairness
>
> Leadership

Temperance

Forgiveness

Self-control

Humility

Caution

Transcendence, or connection with an enduring sense of meaning

Appreciation

Gratitude

Humor

Spirituality

Hope

Seligman isn't suggesting that any of these strengths or groups of strengths is superior to others. He is simply identifying common values that people all over the world find important to some degree.

Seligman believes that each of us has a group of five of strengths, or values, that are stronger than the others. These are our character strengths. If you go to http://www.authentichappiness.sas .upenn.edu, you'll find a self-test, with 240 multiple-choice questions, that will give you your own profile (the VIA Survey of Character Strengths); another option is the Brief Strengths Test, with just twenty-four questions. Both are free, and you'll get your results immediately. As of 2011, almost two million people had taken the test. Those who subsequently did some of the follow-up activities on the Authentic Happiness website became happier and less depressed (Seligman et al. 2005).

Researchers have found that using our character strengths can reduce stress and boost our sense of being fully alive. In one study, researchers found that "people who reported greater use of the strengths developed greater levels of well-being over time" (Wood et al. 2011, 17). Using your own character strengths will increase both the number and quality of positive experiences in your life. Using them on the job will increase your job satisfaction and general sense of well-being. Those who use their strengths regularly report being in a state of flow more often and having more genuine self-esteem. Why? Because, going back to Fredrickson's theory, using our strengths— staying true to our core values—broadens our perspective and builds our resources.

My five top strengths are kindness, leadership, creativity, love of learning, and appreciation of beauty and excellence. When I'm confronted with a problem or challenge, these are the strengths that will help me the most. What are yours?

1. _____

2. _____

3. _____

4. _____

5. _____

Now, go back to the exercise in chapter 2 in which you identified your top five values. Not surprisingly, you'll probably find that your character strengths are much the same.

Use Your Character Strengths

Get out your calendar and set aside time, at least three times per week, to give one or more of your character strengths some exercise. This will both reinforce the strength and make you happier. Whenever possible, do your best to find ways to use strengths that connect you more with others. For example, if one of your strengths is appreciation of beauty, go to a concert or art exhibit with a friend. If one of your strengths is social intelligence, make time to get together with people you don't know very well but would like to know better. If spirituality is in your top five, make sure to make a space in your life for meditation or prayer. Commit to doing this for at least two weeks.

What will you do to give your character strengths a workout this week?

1. _____

2. _____

3. _____

What will you do to give your character strengths a workout next week?

1. _____

2. _____

3. _____

At the end of the two weeks, return to this exercise and write about your experience, or at least make some notes. Writing things down makes us focus and really think about how an experience affected us. I've provided space here to write about one experience. Please do keep a journal and write about other times when you use your character strengths. (For a downloadable version of this form, visit http://www.newharbinger.com/31021; see the back of the book for information on how to access it.)

What I did: _____

How doing it made me feel: _____

_____

How doing it helped me: _____

_____

Once the two weeks are up, I encourage you to continue doing this activity. Building genuine self-esteem takes some work. The people who report more sustained happiness and a greater reduction of depression and anxiety are those who stick with it.

When one of my students who's a musician asked me to attend one of her concerts, I agreed, at first because my student is far from home and doesn't have a family member nearby who can go and applaud her efforts. I guess you could say I was working from my character strength of kindness. What I realized later was that it also put me back in touch with my appreciation of beauty. As a busy working mom, I'd stopped going to concerts years ago. I just never seemed to find the time. Meanwhile, there's a banquet of good music and art at the university, less than a mile from my house. In my overly busy life, I had forgotten that. My student's invitation got me back into the habit of enjoying great music played by talented young musicians. Taking just a couple of hours to attend a concert every month or so has enriched my life immeasurably.

When I think about how going to concerts regularly increases my positivity, I immediately go back to PERMA: It's a *positive* experience. I'm *engaged* with something that's important to me. It enhances my *relationship* with my student and with the people I bring to concerts with me. It gives *meaning* to my life. The only element that's missing is *achievement*. Of course, all activities won't hit all five pillars of positive psychology. I'd say four out of five is fine!

Engage with Problems

People who survive and thrive don't avoid their problems; they engage with them. They don't sit around wishing things would get better; they keep functioning in spite of the difficulties. Needless to say, doing so usually takes courage.

The route out of learned helplessness is to start working on problems. Even a small success can give us the traction we need to keep going. Engagement doesn't necessarily mean we'll solve the issue right away. It isn't always rewarded. But courage helps us keep at it.

Identify three problems or issues in your life that you'd like to solve or at least improve, then rank order them 1, 2, and 3, from easiest to hardest. Start with the easiest. (I'm a great believer in creating successes for ourselves by starting with what's easy.) Now get busy. What's one small step you can take to make just a little progress? Move through the problem, step by small step. Then do the same for the other two problems. As you complete each step, check it off and give yourself permission to feel good about every little accomplishment. By tackling problems one small step at a time, you can cut them down to a manageable size and experience some success along the way. Soon even big problems will seem more solvable. (If you'd like to continue using this approach for other problems, or if you need more space for a particular problem, you'll find a downloadable form at http://www.newharbinger.com/31021.)

Problem 1: _____

Small steps for making positive changes:

_____ 1. _____

_____ 2. _____

_____ 3. _____

_____ 4. _____

_____ 5. _____

_____ 6. _____

Problem 2: _____

Small steps for making positive changes:

_____ 1. _____

_____ 2. _____

_____ 3. _____

_____ 4. _____

_____ 5. _____

_____ 6. _____

Problem 3: _____

Small steps for making positive changes:

_____ 1. _____

_____ 2. _____

_____ 3. _____

_____ 4. _____

_____ 5. _____

_____ 6. _____

Count the Good Stuff

Remember, the negativity bias, or tendency to focus on everything that's wrong, is very much part of being human. There's certainly plenty to feel negative about. Just watch the first ten minutes of network news. Sure, it's important, as my grandmother said, to know what's going on in the world: to be informed about approaching storms, current dangers in our communities, and what's happening in the economy. All of those things contribute to our decisions about how best to take care of ourselves. But if we focus primarily on the bad and worrisome stuff without some attention to what's right and good for balance, our ability to feel good and do good takes a hit.

You may be old enough to remember the Irving Berlin song about the healing powers of counting our blessings instead of counting sheep when we're worried and can't sleep. He was onto something. Positive psychologists often suggest doing something similar as an antidote to all of the negativity we may encounter each day. While it's an old-fashioned idea and can seem Pollyanna-ish if not done thoughtfully, reminding ourselves of the good things that are happening and what's going right can gives us the vision and strength to carry on.

Below, you'll find a form for recording three positive things that happen each day. Because I advocate doing this as an ongoing practice, you might want to use a separate piece of paper or small journal. (You'll also find a downloadable form for this purpose at http://www.newharbinger. com/31021.) Whatever you use, keep it in a place where you'll remember to use it every day: Next to your bed? Where you have coffee every morning? On your desk? Make a commitment to take five minutes every day to record three positive things that happened to you in the last twenty-four hours.

These don't have to be earthshaking events like winning the lottery or a marriage proposal, although such things could certainly be on the list. Most good things are much smaller but still quite meaningful. Maybe a coworker recognized that you went above and beyond. Perhaps you got a supportive comment on your Facebook page or a good friend called just to catch up. Or maybe you found something you'd been looking for for days. Our lives are full of these little moments of positivity if we just look for them. If you really can't think of anything, you can always be thankful that you're alive, that you have electricity in your house, and that you're fortunate to be able to take a shower. It's easy to take such things for granted. Feeling good is often made up of countless tiny things. We just have to notice them.

To enhance this practice, also write down how you may have helped make these positive moments happen. Some are simply gifts from the sky. But others are a consequence of something you did. By recording your role in making good things happen, you can empower yourself to build the doing part of genuine self-esteem.

Try it now. Write down three positive things from the last twenty-four hours.

1. _____

How I helped make it happen: _____

_____

2. _____

How I helped make it happen: _____

_____

3. _____

How I helped make it happen: _____

_____

Make a commitment to keep track of three good things that happen every day for the next couple of weeks and see how you feel. Then, during times when you feel down or discouraged, you can go back through your entries to remind yourself that good things do happen in your life, and that you play a role in making them happen.

Keep Things in Perspective

One of the most inspiring things I read in the past year wasn't in a philosophy or psychology book. It was an interview with Michael J. Fox in an old *Good Housekeeping* magazine I picked up while waiting in the dentist's office (Fox 2013). You're probably familiar with the actor from his roles in the Back to the Future movies and the TV show *Spin City*. You may also be aware that he's been dealing with Parkinson's disease for almost twenty years. Parkinson's is a debilitating progressive disease that causes shaking and trembling, muscle stiffness, slow movements, and problems with balance. Nonetheless, Fox is a poster child for positivity. He continues to embrace life and use his talents. In 2013 he started a new TV series, *The Michael J. Fox Show*, in which he largely plays his funniest version of himself—a self with Parkinson's.

How does he do it? He has a unique perspective. In interviews, he often tells a story about a woman in labor who was caught in a flood. To save her baby, she climbed a tree and gave birth there. Fox says that whenever one of his children has a complaint, he says, "A lady had a baby in a tree—whaddya got?" It's his family's code for "Let's keep this in perspective." Few things are as bad as we make them out to be.

Think of something negative that has happened in your life in the last few weeks (or maybe that is happening right now). Make a few notes about it here:

Now think about it. Is it as bad as having a baby in a tree during a flood? It's crucial to our sense of well-being (and our health) to be able to separate an inconvenience from a crisis, and to be able to separate a small crisis from a big one.

> Phil came into my office incensed. He'd been waiting all morning for what he thought was an important piece of mail. He'd forgotten that it was a federal holiday so mail wouldn't be delivered. He ranted. He swore. He made his blood pressure go up and scared the people in the next room. Yes, it was inconvenient. But the mail would come the next day, right? I wanted to say, "A lady had a baby in a tree, Phil. Chill."

Reframe the Bad Stuff

One way to maintain a healthy perspective is through what's called *reframing*. That means finding the positives even in the midst of events that feel difficult or even traumatic. It's similar to what we do when taking a photo. If we don't quite like what we see in the viewfinder, we move the camera until we've got the picture we want. The same can be true in life. If you don't like how you're seeing something, move the frame.

Here's an example: Say you clean the house thoroughly before your mother-in-law comes to visit. Within minutes of her arrival, she starts sponging down your fridge. You might frame this as her being critical of your housekeeping. A reframe would be understanding that she's as anxious around you as you are around her. Shining up the fridge is her way of calming her anxiety. If that's the case, the solution becomes obvious. Instead of being angry that she's so critical, you have room to be compassionate and try to think of another way for her to be less nervous around you. (Or you could just let her do it and thank her. She gets to work off her anxiety. You get a shinier fridge. Everyone wins.)

Reframing isn't intended to be a way to avoid issues or make light of problems. It's a way to shift our focus and perhaps open up new possibilities. Often it's also a way to recognize our hidden strengths. For example, if you were a victim of abuse, you could focus on the victimization, or you could focus on the fact that you're still standing. There was some core of strength that helped you through. That doesn't negate the fact that you were victimized. But acknowledging your strength is an important first step that can help you move from identifying yourself as a victim to identifying yourself as a survivor.

Think of a couple of problems that you're trying to solve. Then, for each, change the frame. See the problem from another point of view or in a way that's kind.

Problem 1: _____

Reframe it: _____

_____

Problem 2: _____

Reframe it: _____

_____

Now describe a few ways that reframing each problem opens up new options or solutions.

New options for problem 1:

_____

_____

_____

New options for problem 2:

_____

_____

_____

Do Random Acts of Kindness

You've probably heard or seen the phrase "Practice random kindness and senseless beauty." For a while, I saw this on bumper stickers everywhere. I'm sorry the sticker went out of style. In my experience, doing these kinds of things is associated with improved mood, even several months after people do them.

Positive psychologists often make this simple prescription: practice at least three random acts of kindness or senseless beauty each day. To this, I would add make sure these acts are in line with your values. By actively seeking out opportunities to add kindness and beauty to the world, we activate the doing half of genuine self-esteem. (By the way, if you want to improve your relationship with your partner, sending several small acts of kindness in his or her direction every day will do wonders.)

Here are a few ideas to get you started:

- Let someone who's buying only a few items go ahead of you in the checkout line.

- Let someone else have that parking space that's closer to the store.

- Let someone who's been trying to turn get through a long line of traffic.

- Say please and thank you to waitstaff.

- Tip generously.

- Hand out compliments—sincerely and often.

- Let people at work know you appreciate their efforts.

Now think about acts that appeal to you and fit your values. Add them to the list. Brainstorm six random acts of beauty and kindness and commit to doing them over the next week:

1. _____

2. _____

3. _____

4. _____

5. _____

6. _____

Be sure to do these acts even if you don't feel like it at the time—in fact, especially if you don't feel like it. You can take a page from the exercise Act "As If," in chapter 4. Doing good is likely to kick-start you into feeling good, or at least better.

Make a Bragging Box

A bragging box is a place to store things that remind you of your strengths: thank-you notes, certificates of appreciation, cards you've received, and other objects that remind you of successes that were meaningful to you. If you're creative, which I'm not, you could decorate a shoebox. Me? I simply have a file, which I keep in front of the bills and other unpleasant things. Gretchen Rubin, on the other hand, is definitely creative. In her book *The Happiness Project* (2009), she describes making a Happiness Box where she stores all kinds of little mementos that trigger happy memories and thoughts.

For the sake of genuine self-esteem, which is about doing as much as feeling, I'd suggest adding objects that remind you of things you did well. My file has thank-you notes from students and colleagues, an employee of the month certificate, and a couple of certificates I earned for completing trainings that were particularly challenging. I've got a map of Germany in there to celebrate times when I've been able to make friendly connections with people there—in spite of only speaking German like a three-year-old. There are postcards of fine paintings from museums I've visited. Pictures of my kids are included, both for the glow of pride they give me, and to remind me that my husband and I must have done some things right at least some of the time because our kids are all good people. I also cherish an anniversary card from my husband as a celebration of forty-five years of being loved and mostly being worthy of it.

Brainstorm some of the things you could put in your bragging box:

_____

_____

_____

_____

_____

Now create a bragging box, even if it's only a file folder, and start filling it up. Its contents will be a collection of tangible reminders that you know how to be good and do good. On days when you're down or troubled, you can take them out and savor them. If you let yourself truly appreciate everything they represent, you'll be energized and better able to face whatever problems or difficulties come your way.

Pay It Forward

Recently, I saw a "making a difference" segment of an evening network news show that featured people who were quite literally paying it forward. A growing trend in American communities is for people in fast-food drive-up lines to pay for the order of the person behind them. One restaurant owner who was interviewed said that he's no longer surprised by it because it happens several times a week at his place. The person who pays feels good about making someone's day. The person who receives the unexpected gift is delighted.

Paying it forward means repaying a kindness or good deed by passing it on to someone else instead of the original donor. Catherine Ryan Hyde wrote a novel called *Pay It Forward* (1999), which was later made into a popular movie. She founded the Pay It Forward Foundation, which is dedicated to creating a ripple effect of kind acts around the world.

There are lots of ways to pay it forward to pass along a kindness. One of the best things a friend ever did for me happened when I was mothering three young children. She dropped in one day and said, "Take a nap. I'll watch the kids for a couple hours." A worry-free break to get some needed sleep was worth more to me at that time than gold. Now that my kids are grown, I look for ways to assist young moms when I can. I know from experience what a relief it is to get a little help.

Think of some of the times when you've been the recipient of a good deed. Are there ways you can pass it on? Write a few of your ideas here:

_____

_____

_____

Now go for it! That's what the doing part of genuine self-esteem in all about. Paying it forward will feel good and will add to your sense of connection with others.

Thank Yourself

Remember the negativity bias? It's that all-too-human tendency to focus on the negative. Always looking for ways to improve, we forget to give ourselves appreciation for all the things we're doing to keep ourselves healthy, strong, and happy. For those in despair, even getting up in the morning and taking a shower is worth a big thank-you to themselves. It's a start. Whatever our situation, it's important to give ourselves credit for the daily business that supports the busyness: eating reasonably well, getting to the gym for some exercise (especially when we really don't want to), reading *Goodnight Moon* for the 498th time because our toddler loves it (especially when we're really sick of the story), remembering to hug our partner, call our mother, buy candles for a birthday cake, and on and on. All of these little and not so little efforts are the emotional and practical grease that keeps life running smoothly.

So take a moment to thank yourself for everything you've done today. No, this isn't silly. It's important. Recognizing the positives in life—what's going well—provides the energy we all need if we're to address things that do need improvement.

Dear Self,

Today I very much appreciate that you _____

_____

_____

_____

_____

_____

_____

_____

_____

Sincerely,
Me

Write a Letter Forgiving Someone

Forgiveness is acknowledging and dealing with it when someone has done you wrong. This isn't venturing into negativity, and it isn't about letting someone off the hook for doing something hurtful. Forgiveness doesn't require the other person to agree with you or apologize, even though that might be appropriate. It isn't intended to allow you to continue to accept bad treatment. If you're being treated badly, get out of the situation! The point of forgiveness is that it gives you a way to stop dwelling on wrongs and move past them. Holding on to anger, bearing a grudge, plotting revenge, or feeling diminished by someone else's actions are all toxic to you. Forgiving is a way to let all of this go.

Former South African president Nelson Mandela is a role model for us all. He once spoke with Hillary Clinton about being freed after eighteen years of wrongful imprisonment. He told her, "As I walked out the door toward the gate that would lead to my freedom, I knew if I didn't leave my bitterness and hatred behind, I'd still be in prison" (Clinton 2004, 236).

Think of someone you feel wronged you in the past: _____

Describe what that person did, being as specific as you can be:

_____

_____

_____

How did it make you feel?

_____

_____

What could you honestly say to offer forgiveness? If you can't forgive the entire event, find something the person said or did that you can forgive. It may help to consider what might have caused the person to behave in that way and to summon compassion for whatever led to the behavior. Now write a forgiveness letter in the space provided or, if you need more, write or type it on a separate piece of paper.

Date:_____

Dear _____,

_____

_____

_____

_____

_____

_____

_____

Sending the letter isn't required unless you think it could provide a new beginning in your relationship. If you think or know that it would invite more abuse or start an argument, throw the letter away. You don't want to open up old wounds or make the situation worse.

How did you decide whether or not to send your letter? What values did you prioritize in making that decision?

_____

_____

_____

The forgiveness letter isn't really for the other person. It's for you. It's a way to get rid of some of the negativity you may be carrying around and make more room for positive feelings.

Record your reactions to this activity while they're still fresh:

_____

_____

_____

_____

Remember What This Is All About

Remember, genuine self-esteem has two parts that reinforce and support each other. To live comfortably in quadrant 3, we need to feel good about ourselves and we need to do good things to deserve that feeling. Self-compassion lets us let go of blame and shame so we can make a new start. By increasing our ratio of positive to negative emotions to at least three to one, we broaden our ability to see more options for our lives and build our resources for solving problems. We feel good and become more capable of doing good. By using our character strengths and by doing activities like those in this chapter, we build on what's already strong within us to increase all five of the principles of positive psychology expressed in the acronym PERMA: positive feelings, engagement, relationships, meaning, and achievement. As Barbara Fredrickson has pointed out, "Positivity is contagious. Once out there, it spreads" (2009, 69).

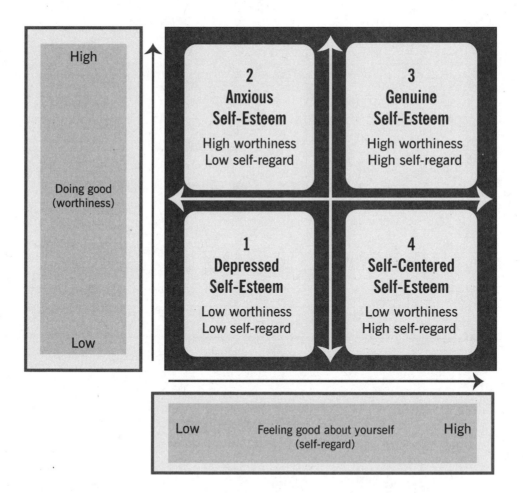

CHAPTER 6

Mindfulness

You do not have to stop the various thoughts and feelings that dawn to the mind; just do not get caught up in them....The mind will then take its own natural form, and the basic purity of its clear light can emerge and be known.

—Dalai Lama

Mindfulness means being present here and now—living in the present moment, rather than getting stuck in the past or lost in the future. It means understanding that thoughts, especially negative thoughts or thoughts about physical or emotional suffering, are just thoughts. They don't have to interfere with our focus, good intentions, or relationships. We can learn to let them rise and fall within us and let them go. By doing so, we can fully relax and appreciate what's happening in the moment, and we become more open and available to other people and more grounded in our daily activities.

In one of his books, the Dalai Lama likens mindfulness to the sea (1998). On top, there may be waves and storms, but those storms don't have much effect deep down. Similarly, a regular practice of meditation can help people develop a deep inner peace that inoculates them from the storms of life and moments of negativity. Difficult events are recognized and felt but don't affect the deeper mind.

That is not to suggest that we shouldn't acknowledge past events or illnesses that have caused us to suffer, nor that we should let go of goals for the future. But by living deeply in the present moment, we can better understand our past, let go of our suffering, and prepare for the future. In addition, when in that relaxed state, the body can marshal its own defenses against pain and disease. By staying tuned in to the here and now, we can develop peace within ourselves (feel good) and add some peace to the world (do good). We can work more fully from quadrant 3— genuine self-esteem. The activities in this chapter will start you on a path toward more mindfulness.

I was introduced to mindfulness about forty-five years ago when my husband's brother stopped by our house, bubbling over with enthusiasm. With hair to his waist and wearing frayed jeans, a leather vest, and sandals, David could have been the poster boy for the 1960s. (He later became a classical singer of Bach cantatas, but that's another story.) He had just returned from being instructed in a kind of meditation. He loved it! For my highly anxious brother-in-law, learning how to turn down the scolding in his head and find moments of calm was a huge relief. He wanted to share his discovery with me. He encouraged (no, badgered) me to start a meditation practice to ease stress and find enlightenment. At that time, I was highly skeptical about most enthusiasms brought to me by my much loved but often over-the-top brother-in-law, so I passed on his offer to teach me, then soon forgot all about it as I turned my attention to other things, like the stressful task of finishing my graduate studies. Yes, I know. If I'd taken him up on the offer, I could have done my schooling with a lot less stress.

Fast-forward a decade. I got over my skepticism about mindfulness as I watched its positive effects on David and others I knew. Once I gave it a try, I kicked myself for not being more open to it sooner. Further, in my search for ways to help clients relieve their stress and anxiety, I discovered that there were important commonalities between various types of meditation, self-hypnosis, and prayer. All involve a momentary surrender of control so that we can be open to compassion and new understanding. As with anything, one size doesn't fit all. Some people find peace in their religion. Some are more comfortable with meditation. Still others prefer self-hypnosis as a way to de-stress and open themselves to something larger. Any regular calming practice can help people stay in the moment as well as detach from and depersonalize stress from both body and mind. Such practices help us remember that there is more to life than the trials of the moment. All are paths to mindfulness.

Why Mindfulness

Sadly, being stressed-out has become the norm for many people in the United States, who tend to carry much too big a load. Contrary to conventional wisdom, being able to multitask isn't always a positive thing. Often it entails frantically juggling responsibilities and tasks to the point of exhaustion. As stress increases, quality of life takes a nosedive. People start to fall apart both psychologically and physically. They are irritable with their coworkers, families, and friends. Their genuine self-esteem takes a big hit. It's hard to feel good or do good when we feel anxious, stressed to the max, and overwhelmed.

Over the last few decades, mindfulness has emerged as a way to address the epidemic of stress and the variety of mental and physical disorders it can create. It's a new application of a very old Buddhist technique—with an important difference or addition. In Buddhism, mindfulness is seen as a path to enlightenment. In modern psychology and medicine, it's seen as a path to reduced stress, better health, and better quality of life. Of course, both can be true. But it's important to draw the distinction. You need not be a Buddhist to benefit from being more mindful. Here, we'll take a look at a few of the people who have been instrumental in making mindfulness available to all of us.

Herbert Benson was one of the first scientists to start researching how to utilize mindfulness in medicine. In the 1960s, he and his team discovered that humans have an innate ability to counter the fight-or-flight response that heightens anxiety and creates physiological stress. He named that healing ability the *relaxation response* (Benson and Klipper 1975). He found that by simply getting comfortable, breathing slowly and steadily, and saying the word "one" over and over, people can relax the body and ease the mind. In this relaxed state, the body can better utilize its own defenses.

Although the relaxation response doesn't have a spiritual component, Benson acknowledges that the same response has been elicited for centuries through such practices as meditation, yoga, prayer, and even spiritual dance and song. The common denominator among all such techniques is repetition of something—a word, sound, movement, or prayer—to the exclusion of all other thoughts. When thoughts intrude, the mind is directed back to the focus on repetition and the body relaxes. Benson's relaxation response achieves the same thing.

You may have heard of another American doctor and professor, Jon Kabat-Zinn, who has also been advocating the use of mindfulness to ease pain, illness, stress, and anxiety for decades. He developed an eight-week program called mindfulness-based stress reduction (MBSR) and has focused his research efforts on measuring its effectiveness, as well as studying the mind-body connection more generally. MBSR helps people who are chronically ill or in pain get relief by gaining more balance and peace of mind through mindfulness meditation and yoga. Both Benson and Kabat-Zinn have demonstrated that mindfulness can reduce pain in medical conditions like immune disorders, fibromyalgia, and heart disease, to name just a few, as well as symptoms of anxiety and depression (Benson 1993; Kabat-Zinn 1993).

Thich Nhat Hanh, a Zen Buddhist monk and peace activist, has probably done more than anyone to bring the practice of mindfulness to mainstream America. Through workshops, retreats, and classes, as well as over one hundred books (forty in English), he has touched the lives of thousands.

I was privileged to attend one of his retreats several years ago at a local college. Hundreds of people came and listened with rapt attention. Some were brought to tears by simply being there. Others responded with joy and laughter. He said some very wise things, but I think his calm approach to life's problems is what people found compelling. Clearly he was someone who knew how to manage a complicated life without drama or stress. Instead, he radiated peace and grace. Whatever gave him that, people wanted more of it!

Researcher Kristin Neff's idea of self-compassion echoes the teachings of Thich Nhat Hanh and the Dalai Lama. And all of these figures ask us to embrace our suffering as a connection to the human condition. When we feel that oneness with others and realize that we are experiencing a poignant part of being human, we can stop judging ourselves. Then we can be kinder to both ourselves and others and let go of our suffering. Our genuine self-esteem grows because we can feel good and do good. Nelson Mandela drew the same conclusion, reflected in this statement: "Our human compassion binds us the one to the other—not in pity or patronizingly, but as human beings who have learned how to turn our common suffering into hope for the future" (2012, 24).

Obstacles to Mindfulness

Countless times, I've heard "yes, but" when I've introduced the idea of mindfulness to friends or clients. Some objections are grounded in mistaken ideas about what mindfulness is. Others are due to anxieties about letting go of what's familiar and trying something that, for some people, is a new, very different approach to managing stress.

Thinking Mindfulness Is Just a Fad

Over the last decade, mindfulness has shown up on bumper stickers and Facebook, appeared in the plots of TV sitcoms, and been the subject of daytime talk shows. It's understandable that some people might wonder whether this is a fad or if there's actually something to it. If it's a fad, it's had an extremely long run. Cultures across Asia have been practicing some version of mindfulness for centuries and, in some cases, millennia. That's not to say that millions of people who have done something for thousands of years can't be wrong, but it does support the idea that people find it helpful.

Thinking Mindfulness Is Too "New Age"

Some of us are still recovering from the human potential movement's excesses in the 1970s. Mindfulness can look too "new age" and maybe a little flaky. Thinking about it brings visions of people sitting in the lotus position, examining their navels, and chanting "om" rather than being realistic and doing what needs to be done.

It's important to separate the deeply meaningful practice of mindfulness from any superficial interpretations of Eastern thought and practice we may have seen. People can sit in the lotus position while meditating if they want to, but it isn't necessary. We can be mindful while we walk to work, do household chores, or simply relax in a comfortable chair. The object isn't to withdraw from our responsibilities; it's to withdraw from stress, allowing us to more easily accept and deal with those responsibilities.

> When I first introduced the idea of meditation to Katie, she didn't want anything to do with it. "Oh that's so Valley," she said, referring to the fact that seemingly every possible type of new age and alternative treatment is available in the valley where we both live. But Katie had serious back pain. Numerous medical interventions hadn't helped, so her primary care physician recommended that she come to me for pain management. After I suggested that giving meditation a try wouldn't cost her anything except a half hour of her life, she agreed—with a shrug and a "Why not?" She was surprised to find that just one session gave her some relief.

Being Uncomfortable with "God Talk"

Alcoholics Anonymous has been a successful self-help program for many people. One of the fundamental threads in the program is looking to a higher power for help. Some people can't tolerate the "god talk" and therefore miss out on what the program might offer them. This is unfortunate and self-limiting. After all, a relationship with something larger than ourselves can take many forms besides organized religion, including a connection with nature or the cosmos, or humanism. Mindfulness is rooted in ancient Buddhist spiritual traditions, so you may have similar concerns about it. However, being mindful doesn't require talking about or even acknowledging our spirituality. We are only asked to accept that compassion and kindness are available to all of us. According to Jon Kabat-Zinn, "Perhaps the most 'spiritual' thing any of us can do is simply to look through our own eyes, see with eyes of wholeness, and act with integrity and kindness" (2005, 270).

Being Concerned That It Competes with One's Religion

Mindfulness doesn't compete with any other form of spiritual practice. If your religious or spiritual practice is dear to you and brings you closer to God or your higher power, you may not need mindfulness at all. Prayer, when done thoughtfully and deeply, can be seen as a type of meditation. On the other hand, perhaps you'd like to consider enjoying the benefits of both.

In his talks, Thich Nhat Hanh often draws this analogy: If your favorite fruit is mango, that doesn't mean you can't also eat or enjoy other fruits, such as banana or pineapple. Liking other fruits doesn't take anything away from your favorite. Nhat Hanh tells us to honor our religious roots, whatever they may be. It's fine to enjoy the peace and teachings that come from more than one tradition.

Losing Sight of Personal Values

Sometimes we get so caught up in all the have-tos that we forget what's really important to us. We start thinking, "When I'm done with _____ , I'll have time to…" or "When I stop being depressed, I'll…." We have good intentions but somehow never get to that elusive future. Practicing some kind of meditation makes us pause during our day and clear our minds of have-tos so we can consider whether there's anything important we might be neglecting while we're so anxiously fixated on checking off items on our to-do list. In that calm space, we can reconsider whether we're making choices that are in line with our core values. In this way, meditation facilitates our genuine self-esteem.

> A friend of mine looks back with regret at his graduate school experience. "I was so focused on finishing my master's thesis that I neglected my friendships and family and didn't do anything in the way of community service or taking care of myself for almost a year. I kept promising myself that nirvana would happen when I got my thesis done. Well, I did finish the thesis, but in the process I gained twelve pounds, missed my grandmother's ninetieth birthday party, skipped out on board meetings of a charity that's important to me, and let down friends who needed a little support from me now and then. When I look back, I realize I could have stayed true to my values if I'd given myself just a few more months to write the thesis. I created my stress. Nobody else did. And I betrayed my own values in the process. I hope I learned.

Being Uncomfortable with Silence

In Western culture, people are constantly moving to background noise, whether they want to or not. Music accompanies our lives in elevators, gas stations, malls, and offices. Young people are constantly plugged into music on their smartphones and tablets. Many homes have a TV or music on in every room at all times. Our cell phones buzz and beep throughout the day. Noise and distraction are so much a part of our lives that many people have become uncomfortable with silence.

Shutting off all of that sound can be uncomfortable at first. Our minds keep up the chatter, especially if we've been using electronic noise to drown out critical and anxious thoughts. But if we can relax into the quiet, we find rest and peace. This is why people go off to the mountains or to beaches (without cell phones) for vacations. Relaxation requires getting away from it all, including electronics.

Mindfulness is much the same as a vacation. Being mindful, and especially meditating, requires shutting off all that sound so we can listen to our own hearts and minds. It means making a space where we can open ourselves to new experience and peace.

Being Resistant to Discipline

For some people, the word "discipline" is negative. They think of being disciplined as being spanked or sent to a time-out. The very idea of a discipline stresses them out. If that's the case for you, please consider this: "Discipline" also refers to being a follower, as in the word "disciple." It can also mean doing something regularly, as in the discipline of practicing a sport, instrument, or fitness routine. Opening ourselves up to learning new things, being disciples, and practicing something in a disciplined way is what helps us grow.

Learning to play the piano or perfecting our backhand in tennis takes more than lessons. We have to practice. The same is true of mindfulness. Once we know how to focus on the present and let go of intrusive thoughts, mindfulness can extend into our day during the course of ordinary events. We can do a walking meditation on our lunch hour, tune in to the beauty of the day as we look out a window, or follow our breath for a few minutes when taking a break at work.

A discipline doesn't have to take up a major part of your day. It's okay to start small. Meditation can be practiced in brief bits of time—say fifteen minutes—a few times a week. To get the most benefit, the important thing is to commit to a "practice," meaning something we do regularly and often.

Mindfulness Self-Assessment

This self-assessment will give you an idea of how mindful you already are. Read through the statements below and, for each, rate yourself using the following scale:

1 = almost never

2 = less than half of the time

3 = about half of the time

4 = more often than not

5 = almost always

_____   It's easy for me to stay focused.

_____   I can turn off negative thinking easily.

_____   I can calm myself when I'm upset.

_____   When I'm down, I can remind myself that this is a human feeling and will pass.

_____   I have compassion for myself as well as for others.

_____   I never tell myself my feelings are bad.

_____   I can sit with silence and let stress fall away.

_____   I'm in touch with how my body feels.

_____   I see myself as being at one with something larger.

_____   It's important to me that I'm able to be in the moment.

_____   I feel connected with the cosmos, other people, and nature.

_____   I can let go of anger, annoyance, and fear through self-compassion.

_____   I notice, really notice, how things taste, smell, and feel.

_____   I'm confident that there's more to life than whatever is bothering me in the moment.

_____   To me, negative thoughts are just thoughts, and I can let them go.

_____   I know that my feelings, both good and bad, are shared by everyone else in the world.

The more items you rated at 4 or 5, the more mindfully you're already living. If you rated most items with a 1 or 2, you might find it helpful to incorporate some kind of meditation practice into your life.

Activity Choices for Increasing Mindfulness

To be mindful simply means to be fully present. There are many ways to become more mindful, but they all boil down to types of meditation. Whether through formal guided meditation or through a disciplined focus while eating, walking, or listening to music, mindfulness can help us stay in the here and now. We can then let go of the stress and pain in our lives. As we become more present and centered, we have more freedom to shift our thinking, feeling, and doing in new and more helpful directions. And we can take that state of calm back to the tasks of life so we can be more effective.

The following activities are based in various forms of meditation and mindfulness, both formal and informal. All of them can help you ease stress and shift your focus to hope, compassion, and loving-kindness for yourself and others. I recommend experimenting with all of them to discover the practices that work best for you.

Also, please be patient. If you're new to it, chances are that getting comfortable with a practice of meditation will take some time. When conducting her Open Heart Study, which examined the results of a seven-week meditation workshop, Barbara Fredrickson found that, on average, people didn't report reliable increases in positive emotions until the third week of meditation practice (2009, 87).

Experience RAIN

Many teachers of mindfulness recommend using the acronym RAIN (recognition, acceptance, investigation, and nonidentification) as a reminder of the essential tools for breaking unconscious habits that prevent us from managing difficult emotions and appreciating the present. Tara Brach, who has taught meditation for over thirty-five years, talks about it in her book *True Refuge* (2013), and Jack Kornfield, another leading meditation teacher, frequently uses it in his retreats and books, including *The Wise Heart* (2009). I love the imagery associated with this acronym. RAIN reminds me of tears, of course. But it also reminds me of cleansing spring rains that help all things grow.

Recognition: Recognize strong emotions as they're happening. Resist the temptation to avoid them, and instead appreciate them as being an important part of the human experience.

Acceptance: Accept your feelings and remember that emotions, even those that are negative, are normal, important, and informative. When you accept your feelings, new possibilities open up.

Investigation: Look deeply into your feelings, your body, and your mind to reach a deeper understanding of your experience.

Nonidentification: Let go of the idea that your emotions define you. See them as useful for information but not permanent.

It's certainly tempting to try to avoid emotional pain. Pain doesn't feel good. In fact, it can feel terrible. But avoiding the pain means also avoiding healing and learning. When we grieve, for example, it's normal to feel sad and angry and wish it would all just go away. But part of the process of grieving is to feel the sadness, acknowledge the anger, and come to terms with the loss. RAIN supports this process so we can get to acceptance of loss and transform it to something good.

Give it a try. Think of a part of your life that's annoying or makes you angry or sad. Identify a specific situation. Imagine it in detail. Now, take yourself through the steps: recognition, acceptance, investigation, and nonidentification. As difficult as it may be, sit with the process for a while. Put this book down and sit quietly. Work through the elements of RAIN for at least twenty minutes, or longer if you need to. Working through emotions takes as long as it takes. When you're finished, or finished enough for now, take a few minutes to write about what you learned:

_____

_____

_____

_____

_____

_____

Follow the Breath

Regardless of teacher or method, awareness of the breath is a primary practice in mindfulness meditation. Here's the basic practice: Find a place where you can sit comfortably. Follow your breathing. Count as you breathe in ("one...two...three"), then count as you breathe out. Some people find that it helps to make the exhale a count or two longer than the inhale. Focus entirely on your breathing and let your thoughts go. Do your best to clear your mind of troubling thoughts, lists of things you have to do, regrets about the past, or anxieties about the future. If you find yourself thinking about anything other than your breath, don't scold yourself. This is natural and common, even among experienced meditators. Just observe that your mind has wandered, then let the thoughts go. You might say to yourself, *I'm thinking about the laundry I have to do, and now I'm letting it go* or *I'm thinking about that problem with my partner, and now I'm letting it go.* Then shift your focus back to quietly inhaling and exhaling.

Don't be surprised or concerned if you tap into deep emotions. Meditating by following the breath sometimes releases deep emotional pain or tension. Some people cry, others laugh, and others find themselves yawning. Such experiences reflect a release of anxiety, tension, sadness, or anger. Let them happen. Don't judge them. As you're able, keep returning to your breath.

As you begin to do this practice, start with relatively brief sessions—just ten to fifteen minutes. Over time, you can increase the duration if you like. However long you practice, give yourself this vacation from stress several times a week. Better yet, do it every day.

After you've practiced a time or two, take a few minutes to write about how following the breath affects you:

_____

_____

_____

_____

_____

_____

_____

Use Guided Meditations

You may have heard of guided meditation. Essentially, you listen to a teacher (in person or via a recording) who coaches you in mindful breathing or takes you though an elaborate imaginary experience. Following the person's voice can help you let go of troubling thoughts and emotional pain, become present, and relax.

Many people find guided meditations extremely helpful when learning to meditate. Others find them distracting because the guidance may clash with their personal experience or own imagination in the course of the meditation. I encourage you to give guided meditation a try to see whether it works for you. Guided meditations are widely available as audio recordings and on YouTube. Experiment to discover which meditations or teachers work well for you. You might also want to look for a local meditation group or retreat where you can experience a guided meditation with a teacher.

Use a Mantra

In Sanskrit, *mantra* refers to a sacred sound, poem, word, or group of words that has spiritual power. Herbert Benson's repetition of "one" to achieve the relaxation response is a secular version. During meditation, a mantra may be repeated over and over again as a point of focus. This repetition helps clear the mind so you can relax. You don't have to say your mantra out loud. You can chant it under your breath or even just think it.

If you use the same mantra consistently, your mind will learn to treat it as an "on" button for meditation. As soon as you start repeating your mantra, you'll settle down, your mind will clear, and you'll ease into a relaxed state. It's a wonderful way to start or end your day or to de-stress whenever you need it. Whether sitting in your own living room or at your office desk, you can take a deep breath and repeat your mantra to yourself for a few minutes as a way to relax and refocus your thoughts and energy.

You may already be familiar with the sound "om" (pronounced "aum"). The vibration of this sound helps many people stay with their meditation. You can use a sound like "om" as your mantra, or you can meditate on a phrase or verse that has meaning for you.

Some people like to use the following verse, from Buddhist monk and teacher Jack Kornfield, as a mantra (2011, 273):

May I be filled with loving-kindness.
May I be safe from inner and outer dangers.
May I be well in body and mind.
May I be at ease and happy.

Others repeat lines from a Bible verse or psalm they like, such as Psalm 19:14:

Let the words of my mouth, and the meditation of my heart,
be acceptable in thy sight, O Lord, my strength, and my redeemer.

Still others like to create their own phrase, verse, or prayer to help direct their thoughts to more positivity and self-care. If you like, write your own meditation mantra here:

_____

_____

_____

_____

Tune In to What Already Is

To be mindful is to be mind-full. It means to fill our minds with the present moment and appreciate where we are and what's around us. One way to do this is to expand a simple sitting meditation to being mindful of our environment by focusing on what we experience through each of the five senses. Read through the following meditation to get the idea (or make an audio recording of it). Then sit comfortably in a chair or on the floor and take a few moments to follow your breath. Breathe in. Breathe out. Slow yourself down. Let your mind become calm.

Now take yourself through each of the five senses:

1. What do you see? Really look at what's around you. You might even break it down further by looking only at things that are a certain color, such as red or green or blue. Breathe in. Breathe out.

2. What do you hear? Tune in to every little noise: the furnace or air conditioner turning on, traffic outside, the buzz of the lamp in your room, or whatever you hear. Breathe in. Breathe out.

3. What do you smell? Concentrate. What aromas can you tease out from the air around you? Breathe in. Breathe out.

4. Is there a flavor in your mouth? Can you still taste the echoes of the last thing you ate? Really tune in to whatever flavors are there. Breathe in. Breathe out.

5. Experience how your body rests against the chair or floor. Sink in more deeply. Tune in to sensations of warmth or coolness and the texture of your clothing,

After first practicing this meditation, take a few moments to write about what you experienced and learned:

_____

_____

_____

_____

_____

_____

Imagine Your Happy Place

Often a good idea shows up in many places, and that's certainly the case with practices that involve visualizing a happy or safe place. When we're stressed, identifying and remembering a time when we were really peaceful and happy can help us get in a better mood and can even decrease the symptoms of depression.

Here's how it goes: Think of a time in the past when you were extremely relaxed and content. Conjure up as complete a memory as you can, calling on all of your senses. Where were you? What did you see? What sounds were there? Can you recall scents or tactile memories, such as the temperature on your skin, softness, or textures? Maybe there are even tastes associated with this situation. Linger in that memory. Really re-create it in your mind and relive how you experienced it with all your senses. Then give the memory a name.

This can become a happy place in your mind. When stressed, depressed, or anxious, all you have to do is sit comfortably, follow your breath for a minute or two, relax, and then call up the name of this place. Focus on the memory and put yourself right back in it. With practice, you'll experience yourself noticeably relaxing in just a few minutes. When you come out, you'll be refreshed and able to focus your energy on what you need to do.

Write a brief description of your happy place here, or make a sketch that will remind you of it on a separate piece of paper.

_____

_____

_____

_____

_____

_____

Practice Walking Meditation

If you find it really difficult to sit still and use only your mind to clear your thoughts, more physically active or sensory forms of meditation may work better for you. By actively focusing on movement or an activity such as walking, eating, or listening to music, you can shift your attention from whatever is troubling you and reduce your level of stress.

I'll start with walking meditation, since many of us spend far too much time at our computers or desks. The truth is, more sitting is the last thing our bodies really need. Walking meditation is entirely different from walking for exercise, where you're trying to get aerobic. Instead, it is slow, considered, and peaceful.

Take yourself on a walk—without a goal of getting anywhere. Instead, focus on the process of moving, feeling each foot connecting with the ground and experiencing your feet bearing your weight. Focus on how one foot rises and then falls. Breathe in. Focus on how it feels to be connected to the earth. Really feel the ground beneath your feet. Then focus on the other foot as you take the next step. Breathe out. Continue walking in this way. You may feel like you're moving in slow motion. Continue to follow your breath and to be aware of your feet touching the ground.

As with sitting meditation, intrusive thoughts will probably arise. When you become aware of them, let them go and redirect your attention to walking. As with the exercise for following the breath, don't be surprised if you become emotional. Walking meditation often releases pent-up tension, emotions, and stress. Don't judge yourself if this doesn't happen. Different people react differently.

After you practice walking meditation the first time, take a few minutes to reflect on what you experienced and learned:

_____

_____

_____

_____

_____

_____

_____

Eat Mindfully

Many people like fast food, eat too much, and eat too fast. Instead of enjoying and savoring food, they inhale it. This often results in eating more in order to feel like they've eaten at all. People take in fewer calories when they eat at a slower pace. Further, slowing down helps us enjoy our meals more. Mindful eating can be an expansive practice that makes us more appreciative of what we have.

It's difficult to know who to attribute the following mindful eating practice to. Thich Nhat Hanh often includes it in his workshops, and it's a foundational practice in Jon Kabat-Zinn's mindfulness-based stress reduction, but I also remember doing something similar many years ago in a workshop run by a Native American healer. Try it once in a while. Staying mindful and in the present moment isn't easy. But when we accomplish it, we clear the mind and experience ordinary acts (like eating a sandwich) in extraordinary ways.

1. Choose a food you really like that's simple to eat. It could be a handful of nuts, a small sandwich, a piece of fruit—anything that's flavorful and that you'll enjoy.

2. Sit down with the food on the table in front of you. Look at it. Take your time. Notice its textures and shapes. When you think you've looked at it enough, look some more. Really take it in.

3. Pick it up. Notice how it feels: its weight, its textures, its firmness. Hold it for a while. Focus on how it feels in your hand.

4. Pick up your food and sniff it as a child would. Take in the aroma.

5. Take a small bite. Chew it slowly. Feel it in your mouth and really taste the flavors. Think about everyone who played a role in bringing this food to you: the farmer, the manufacturer or distributor, the clerk who sold it to you, and so on. Give each of them a moment of thanks.

6. After at least thirty seconds, take another bite. Chew it slowly. Notice how the food tastes. Fully experience how it feels on your teeth and tongue.

7. Continue eating—very, very slowly. Savor the food with gratitude.

When you finish, remain sitting for a few minutes and think about the experience. Remember the sensations. Write about what you experienced:

_____

_____

_____

_____

_____

_____

Obviously, eating meals at this rate could take up your entire day! The point of the exercise isn't to train yourself to eat at a snail's pace. It's just something to do now and then to renew your appreciation for food and pull you into living in the moment. An added benefit is that it can readjust your eating pace if that's an issue for you.

Listen to Music Mindfully

Music can be a great distraction, and depending on the song, it can help us relax or amp us up. This has been recognized since at least the seventeenth century when, in 1697, William Congreve wrote, "Music has charms to soothe a savage breast" in his play *The Mourning Bride* (1840, 237). Current research (Waldon 2001) shows that Congreve was right. Music can reduce pain in cancer patients and ease discomfort for the rest of us as well. That's why so many dentists' offices pipe in music or hand out headphones as soon as we walk in the door. Music activates sensory neural pathways that compete with pain pathways, shifting our focus from pain. The music people find comforting is a matter of individual taste. Some people find classical music soothing and comforting. Others find music with a strong backbeat to be most effective for reducing stress. Play whatever engages your attention, pulls you away from negative thoughts, and lifts your mood.

Listening to music may feel as natural to you as breathing. If so, you already know how it can influence your mood. What kind of music helps you separate from and let go of painful thoughts?

_____

Make a playlist of some of your favorite music to practice listening mindfully. Keep in mind that listening mindfully means more than turning the music on. It requires that you get comfortable, slow down your breathing, and imagine yourself as part of the music.

Try it. Turn on your music. Breathe to the beat or, if the beat is too fast, breathe to every two or four beats. Just settle into a rhythm that lets you relax and keep your focus on the music. Empty your mind of everything else.

After your first session of listening to music mindfully, write about how it made you feel, using as many adjectives as you can think of to describe your experience:

_____

_____

_____

_____

_____

_____

_____

Make Friends with Your Hand

Concentrating and really focusing your attention on anything can be a form of meditation. As Mihaly Csikszentmihalyi wrote, "To pursue mental operations in any depth, a person has to learn to concentrate attention" (1997, 96).

You've undoubtedly heard the expression "I know it like the back of my own hand." But how well do you really know the back of your hand? This activity will help you train your brain to be more focused and in the present while getting to know that hand of yours.

Sit comfortably and rest one hand easily on your lap or a table. Then focus all of your attention on it. Notice the lines, freckles, wrinkles, and veins. Notice the shapes of your fingers and the texture of your skin. Really experience your hand. If you start seeing pictures in it (*Gee, those freckles look like a puppy*), don't get lost in them. Just pull yourself back to studying your hand and let go of any intrusive thoughts that drift through your mind. Get to know your hand so well that you could recognize it if it were among a thousand hands. If your concentration wavers, take a brief mental break but maintain your physical stillness. After a moment, begin again.

If you like this practice and want some variety, you can use any small object as your point of focus. It doesn't matter whether it's an orange, a button, a coin, a rock, or something else. Just make sure it has enough interesting qualities (shapes, colors, and textures) to engage your attention.

After you do this practice for the first time, write about what you experienced and learned.

_____

_____

_____

_____

_____

_____

_____

My client Jossey had symptoms of PTSD. Having grown up with a physically and verbally abusive father, she was hypervigilant and anxious. When people raised their voices, she was immediately triggered into high anxiety. She had worked through a lot of her feelings about the past and was moving toward a positive future, but she couldn't shake her reaction to someone getting loud, even when she absolutely knew it had nothing to do with her. So we worked on it. She learned how to follow her breath to become more calm. She wrote a calming mantra for herself and practiced it. She started her day with a fifteen-minute meditation and also engaged in about five minutes of meditation at lunch and when she first got home from work. She turned on music she loves when stressed. In just a few months, she found that her reactivity had decreased considerably. Once she knew she could manage her feelings, she found that she had fewer intense feelings to manage.

Remember What This Is All About

Remember, genuine self-esteem has two parts that reinforce and support each other. To live comfortably in quadrant 3, we need to have positive self-regard and we need to do things that make us worthy of feeling that way. Mindfulness puts us in touch with our feelings and our environment. It helps us both embrace and let go of our suffering so we can de-stress and move beyond it. It allows us to be compassionate toward ourselves and others as we more fully appreciate that both suffering and joy are important aspects of human experience. When relaxed, we can both feel good and do good by contributing to the positivity in the world. By practicing mindful meditation, we can learn to stay in the present moment and enhance our genuine self-esteem.

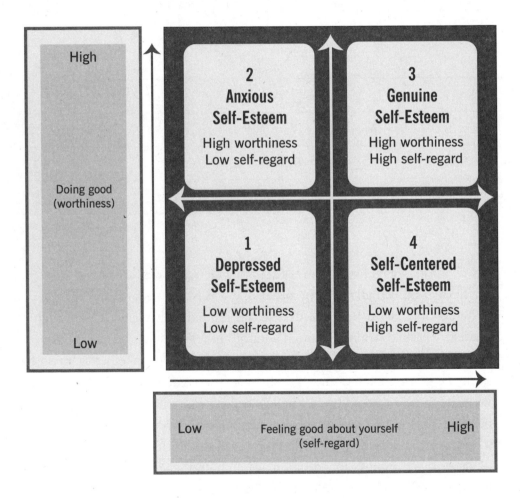

CHAPTER 7

Relationships

We have all known the long loneliness and we have learned that the only solution is love and that love comes with community.

—Dorothy Day

By now, you know the drill: in order to have genuine self-esteem, we have to do good as well as feel good. This can't happen in a social vacuum. Someone has to be on the receiving end of all that good doing. Relationships, then, are central to having genuine self-esteem. We feel good when we give quality time to a family member or friend, help or acknowledge someone, or contribute to the positive feel of our larger community. What comes back is a general sense of belonging, and perhaps a more specific return of personal attention and support.

Living in quadrant 3, genuine self-esteem, means embracing the fact that we are, by nature and by need, social creatures. We need each other not only to survive difficult times but also to share in the good. In this chapter, we'll look at how to enhance personal and community connections and how doing good for others benefits us as well.

My friend Ester is a walking example of the relationship aspect of genuine self-esteem. Her motto is "Never lose a friend." She stays in touch with four women she went to elementary school with over thirty years ago. She uses social media to keep track of college classmates and former colleagues from various jobs. If someone is sick or troubled, she's one of the first people there with homemade soup or an offer to run an errand. Her husband of ten years is her biggest fan. When asked how she does it, Ester is genuinely mystified. To her, staying in touch with people is what life is all about. And what goes around comes around: When Ester was seriously ill a couple of years ago, one of her friends was able to organize Ester's circle of friends to bring her meals and help out with chores for a month. When she recovered, over fifty people had a party to celebrate. Ester has built a strong and connected network of people who are there for each other. She is living a life of genuine self-esteem.

The Importance of Connections

One of the funny things about humans is that we seem to need to rediscover the same truths over and over again. The ancient Greek philosopher Aristotle is said to have taught that the best way to be happy is to help others be happy. Fast-forwarding to the early decades of the twentieth century, Alfred Adler repeatedly taught that the measure of mental health is the degree to which we feel a sense of belonging with others. In the same way, Thich Nhat Hanh's teachings call on us to understand that our suffering is not ours alone; that we are one with everyone who suffers, and also at one with everyone's experience of joy. Martin Seligman and other positive psychologists see relationships as one of the five pillars of positive self-esteem (remember the R in PERMA). Every major thinker and researcher I've talked about in this book believes that connectedness is central to well-being. People are happiest when they do acts of kindness for others. Having good friends and a strong sense of belonging to a larger community are both at the core of genuine self-esteem.

Songwriters, as well as philosophers, psychologists, and monks, understand our need for one another. Most of the songs in the Top 40 are about needing someone, the sadness of losing someone, or the joy of finding someone. Although the majority of the songs are about lovers, there are also many touching and uplifting songs about the value of friendships. You're likely to hear about the importance of friends on almost any radio station, regardless of the genre of music played: *You've Got a Friend*, by Carole King; *I'll Stand by You*, by The Pretenders; *Stand By Me*, by Ben E. King; *Anytime You Need a Friend*, by Mariah Carey; *Friends in Low Places*, by Garth Brooks; *You've Got a Friend in Me*, by Randy Newman; and on and on. Such songs are anthems to the importance of connections in our lives, reminding us that being a good friend is one of the joys of life.

Dunbar's Number

You may wonder how many connections are enough. Robin Dunbar, an evolutionary anthropologist at Oxford University, answers the question in his book *How Many Friends Does One Person Need?* (2010). Don't worry. You don't need a thousand friends. But people generally seem to connect to about 150 people. Dunbar (as well as other researchers) has discovered that the same number—150—is found in widely divergent groups, from the few remaining hunter-gatherer societies to businesses and military units to the communes of the Hutterites (a sect similar to the Amish). It's even true in social media. According to an in-house Facebook study, even people who have five thousand Facebook friends actually interact with (guess how many) about 150. Dunbar theorizes that this has to do with the size of the human brain. But whatever the reason, 150 seems to be about the maximum number of people most of us can honestly say we're connected to.

Of course, the real-life situation is a bit more complicated than just a single number. Imagine a series of concentric circles (like a target) with yourself in the middle. Dunbar has found that people, on average, have an inner ring of three to five good friends. Beyond that lies a ring of about fifteen people who matter a great deal—usually relatives, mentors, and friends who don't quite make the inner circle but still mean a lot. The next ring has about fifty people, typically friends of friends we've gotten to know a bit and people we see regularly but don't count as our own friends. Finally, there's an outer ring of other people we recognize by sight and who are familiar to us. If we were vacationing somewhere and ran into them, we'd recognize each other and say hello. If you're active in your community, you probably have more connections than you think you do—probably about 150!

All of the rings are important. It's our sense of belonging to a larger community, as well as having a few close friends, that makes us feel safe. The folks in our inner rings are the people who are part of our immediate daily lives. We call on each other in times of need and rejoice with each other when there are reasons to celebrate. We do good for each other and feel good for doing it. Moving outward through the rings, we can still do good things and feel good about it through more general actions, like just being friendly. In times of crisis, people from all the rings tend to pull together to save each other and their community as a whole.

Relationships Make Us Healthy

We generally feel better, and feel better about ourselves, when we're connected. Researchers at Brigham Young University studied data from 148 previously published studies that measured how human interactions impact health. They found that social connections improve a person's odds for survival by about 50 percent (Holt-Lunstad, Smith, and Layton 2010).

Conversely, John Cacioppo, a pioneer in the field of social neuroscience, found that loneliness can actually make us sick (Cacioppo and Patrick 2009). It seems that when we're lonely, genes linked to inflammation are overexpressed, while genes linked to antiviral responses are suppressed. Further, Cacioppo reports that loneliness can lead to sleep problems, elevated blood pressure, increase in the stress hormone cortisol, and a diminished sense of living a meaningful life.

Relationships Keep Us Happy

Having good health and living to one hundred wouldn't be much fun if we weren't happy along the way. It turns out that friends, especially happy friends, help each other be happy. We feel good when we're together, and we're happy to do things for each other. In an especially striking study, researchers delved into data from 4,739 individuals in the famous Framingham Heart Study. They found that not only health but also happiness and well-being are dependent on social networks. Happy people tend to be found in the middle of a social network of similarly happy people. Not only that, but our happiness is associated with the happiness of people at up to three degrees of separation! That means that if friends of friends of your friends are generally happy, you're likely to be happy too (Fowler and Christakis 2008). Incidentally, it also works the other way. People who are unhappy spread their unhappiness and negative habits. It stands to reason, then, that adding to the happiness of the world by being happy and positive with friends and other people—in other words, doing good—is central to our genuine self-esteem. It's also a major factor in making our world a better (and happier) place in which to live.

Relationships Are Mutually Protective

Fred Rogers, known by millions of fans from his TV show *Mister Rogers' Neighborhood*, used to tell this story: "When I was a boy and I would see scary things in the news, my mother would say to me, 'Look for the helpers. You will always find people who are helping'" (2003, 187). His mother was right. I'll go one step further and say that people who have genuine self-esteem are often first on the scene when help is needed. They don't have to think about it; they just do it. And by doing good, they immediately start helping those around them feel a little bit better.

It's said that it takes a village to raise a child. The truth is, it takes a village to keep us all safe, healthy, and happy. Our challenge is to become part of our village in a meaningful way. In addition to seeking out the helpers when we need comfort or practical help, we need to develop ourselves so that we can stand among them.

Eliot is a therapist friend of mine. When a tornado went through our area a couple of years ago, entire neighborhoods were flattened. I was able to reach Eliot on his cell phone. "How are things going?" I asked. He replied, "We'll be okay. My folks live across town and can put us up while we figure it out, but there are lots of people milling around just kind of shocked." When I asked if crisis counselors had come in yet, he said, "Yeah, but people don't want to sit with a stranger to talk about it. Not yet anyway." He then said something I'll never forget: "I went out and got some hamburgers and set up my grill. People are able to talk when they're getting fed." Here was a guy who just had a tree fall on his house, and he was out there grilling burgers and using his therapy skills to help his neighbors. If you had asked him why he was feeding people, he might have been stumped. To him, he was doing what was obviously called for: supporting his neighbors in a time of need.

Relationships Keep Us In Touch

I first heard the term "skin hunger" years ago. It struck me then that it was a lovely term to describe the human need for physical touch. I'm not talking about sex (although sex is certainly a wonderful way to be in touch); I'm talking about the intimacy of holding hands or hugging, or a simple touch on the shoulder or stroke on the arm. These small gestures are essential to our sense of security and connection. Without them, we shrivel up emotionally. We know it intuitively, and it's been confirmed scientifically. And yet Americans are among the least touch-oriented people in the world. This is partly due to concerns about being accused of sexual harassment. Partly it's due to our overly busy lives, which reduce our intimate time with people we care about. I'm also sure it partly has to do with electronics that allow us to believe that we're in touch without touching.

Followers of Virginia Satir, one of the "founding mothers" of family therapy, often quote her as saying, "We need four hugs a day for survival. We need eight hugs a day for maintenance. We need twelve hugs a day for growth." Why? Because hugging lets us know that someone thinks we're special enough to hug; because hugging that's welcomed relaxes us and affirms connection with the hugger; because hugs instantly cause our bodies to release oxytocin, sometimes referred to as the cuddle hormone, which bonds parents to children, and friends and partners to each other; because hugging is even thought to strengthen the immune system; and because it feels good!

To be human is to need shared physical contact with other humans. We need at least a few people in our inner Dunbar ring who are comfortable with giving and receiving small gestures of affectionate touching—and big hugs.

> Ninety-year-old Olive loves Fridays. Friday morning is when she and her friends gather at a local hair salon to get their hair done to look good for church on Sunday. The owner, Daryl, is dear to all of them. He provides coffee and doughnuts, and the ladies catch up on the week's doings. When I asked Olive what made her happiest about these Friday morning gatherings, I was moved by her answer: "Oh, Marie. It's the only time now that a man touches me with tenderness and tells me I'm beautiful." How sad and yet how wonderful! Daryl is providing far more than doughnuts.

Obstacles to Connection

We are social by nature and embedded in a social world. We can connect positively by creating and maintaining a variety of types of relationships, from intimate partnerships to acquaintances, or we can relate negatively by being real or virtual hermits. But the fact is, there's no way to not be related to other human beings. Even hermits are still connected, if just by virtue of needing other people to be hermits from! Sadly, people sometimes become discouraged about their ability to participate positively in the human community. Here are some of the most common obstacles to connection.

Lacking Social Skills

Ideally, we learn a variety of social skills in childhood. But those who come from families where people are depressed, chronically negative, addicted, or lacking in social skills themselves don't get that early training. As a result, they don't know how to connect with others and keep the social wheels turning. Feeling awkward and clueless about how it's done, they may be tempted to give up entirely or to pretend they have meaningful online relationships with people they never meet up close and personal. Fortunately, being less than suave socially isn't a terminal disease. Social skills are just that—skills—and skills can be learned. The only thing needed is a teacher.

Isolating Oneself

When people are down, they often want to withdraw from other people. Sadly, it's exactly the wrong thing to do. Being alone too much ultimately leads to being lonely. And when people are lonely, they feel even more down. This can become a vicious cycle. After a while, it can feel like too much effort to leave home, or even the bedroom, and connect with others. At that point, it's not unusual for people to start thinking there's no reason to shower, get dressed, or eat anything better than cold soup straight from the can. They feel they might as well close the curtains and pull the covers over their heads. This may be a way to avoid facing how bad they feel, but it doesn't help them feel better. Self-isolation has never helped anyone break free from depression. Reaching out to a friend, or at least to a professional who can be counted on to be friendly, is a much more effective way to ease back into the social world.

Neglecting Friend Maintenance

Adult life can make it difficult to keep in touch and active in friendships. If we have very full lives, being social as much as we'd like may be on the back burner. It's not that easy to stay in our friends' lives unless we live next door to each other, belong to the same gym, or frequent the same bleachers while watching our kids' games. It's all too easy to let months go by before seeing a good friend face-to-face and sharing something more than a "Hi, how are ya?" on our way to something else.

Keeping friends in a meaningful way requires having some meaningful talks and doing meaningful things together now and then. That means making our friends a priority and making a point to actually get together for lunch, a visit, or a day trip without letting something else get in the way.

> When I told my friend Allen that friendships take work, he vehemently disagreed. "Friendships should be easy," he said. "The whole point of friends is to be able to relax and just enjoy them." But as we continued to talk, Allen realized that he works on his friendships more than he initially thought. He often makes a point of inviting friends who are sports fans to come over and watch important games on TV. He calls people when he hasn't heard from them for a while. He often has lunch with a former professor who has become a friend as well as a mentor. He remembers people's birthdays, at least most of the time. He may not realize it, but he's operating from genuine self-esteem.

Mistaking Quantity for Quality

You can have five hundred "friends" on Facebook and follow another two hundred on Twitter. You can be LinkedIn with hundreds, play an online game with fifty people from all over the world, or engage in online chats with a lot of people you'll never meet. Do these qualify as friends? Yes and no. Yes, they may be part of your larger sense of community. At least some of these people may recognize you and know something about who you are by your "likes" or by the way you present yourself online. They may share strong opinions with you. They might be found in the outer rings of your Dunbar's circles. But they generally aren't people who know you on a complex emotional level or who satisfy your skin hunger.

As Dunbar points out (2010), it's impossible to truly track more than about 150 connections, no matter how many people we friend on Facebook or connect with on LinkedIn. Further, the most important connections occur in our two innermost rings. These are the people we actually spend face time with. They are the people who really know us, warts and all, and love us anyway. They are the people with whom we can have an honest reciprocal relationship, sharing good times and bad, and just sharing. The number is limited not only by the brain, but also by the simple limitations of time. It takes spending time together to foster that kind of depth, and most of us simply don't have enough time in a week or even a month to maintain more than a handful of close relationships.

Being Overdependent

A young man wrote in to my advice column saying, "I've been with my girlfriend since we were sixteen. We both started college this year, and suddenly she's gotten involved with new friends and activities I'm not interested in. She wants to take a break. I can't stand it. She's my everything."

A fifteen-year-old girl wrote with a similar problem: "Me and my two best friends have been together since we were in kindergarten. Now that we're in high school, they've joined up with a group I don't like. I don't know why they're dumping me. I stay in my room and cry every night."

Both of these people let themselves become too dependent on a limited number of relationships. No one can be someone else's "everything." Young lovers sometimes grow apart as they grow up. Friendships can change as people develop new interests or make different life choices. If you're the only person in your group of friends who's married, or if your best friend has kids and you don't, you've been there. Some people can bridge such differences. But some, for a variety of reasons rooted in their own psychology, social skills, or time constraints, just can't.

The solution is to widen our circle. By having a group of friends we can turn to, we won't burn out a particular friend (or a lover) by relying on him or her too much. By sharing our interests with a number of people, we keep our most important relationships fresh and also have a wide network of people to rely on when a relationship or group of friends changes. By spreading our time and energy among a larger group, we can let some relationships go into the background for a while until the situation changes or we can find each other again.

Fearing a Loss of Independence

It's a particularly American idea that in order for people to grow up, they must move away from family and childhood friends. Young people tend to go away to college or move out as soon as they can. Living with family members is seen by some as a disappointment or a defeat, maybe even a sure sign of being a loser. For some people, simply living in the same hometown raises questions of dependency and maturity.

Having negative judgments on Millennials living with their folks is way out of step with the current reality. According to an analysis of US Census Bureau data, in 2012, 36 percent of American young adults ages eighteen to thirty-one were living in their parents' home (Fry 2013). This is the highest percentage in at least four decades. It's even bigger than the 32 percent of young adults who lived with their parents prior to the Great Recession of the late 2000s! While some of these young adults may be suffering from a "failure to launch," there are many good reasons why living with their parents may make good sense. Sometimes young people need to stay put in order to go to college or trade school, to get by on the salary of an entry-level job, or to assist with aging parents. As long as everyone living under the same roof is allowed to be a grown-up, it doesn't have to carry the stigma of "helicopter parenting" or mooching kids.

Living in the same house or geographic area can have many advantages. Family members can help each other with heavy chores, watch each others' kids, share in the care of the elderly, and generally provide a network of love, support, and practical help. In such ways, interdependence can support everyone's genuine self-esteem.

> Marjorie is tired of defending her decision to move into the house next door to her parents. Many of her friends have asked her if she's regressing. "Not at all," she says. She and her husband had tried being totally on their own and found it isn't all it's cracked up to be. Balancing their careers with the demands of raising two lively little boys proved to be an enormous challenge. Multiple child-care solutions had been disappointing: They disagreed with the local day-care center's methods of discipline. Their last three babysitters, though delightful and reliable, had left as soon as they graduated from the local college. A young au pair had wanted to party with friends more than care for the children. Nothing seemed to work happily.

Then the house next door to her parents went on the market. "We talked it over long and hard," says Marjorie. "My mom wanted to take care of the kids during the day, but we didn't want to take advantage. To keep things equal, we're taking on heavier household chores like snow shoveling and yard work that my folks can't do as easily as they used to. It's a major comfort knowing that the person who's taking care of my kids loves them. My folks have been freed of worrying about home maintenance. So far, it's working out fine, probably because my mom and I have always been close."

Disempowering Oneself

When we are overwhelmed and uncertain, it can be tempting to turn decisions over to someone else. Controlling parents, friends, or partners are more than happy to do the job. Although handing decisions over to someone else can help us avoid risk to some extent, it can also set us up to be infantilized, disempowered, or abused. At best, such relationships are a waste of time. At worst, they eat away at our self-respect and trap us in dangerous situations. The better bet is to connect with people who love us and support us in being responsible for our own choices and being our best selves.

Sticking with Negative or Toxic People

Toxic people can be found in any kind of relationship: families, friendships, significant others, colleagues, and even acquaintances. Among them may be a Debbie Downer at work who sucks the joy and energy out of your morning, a narcissistic boss who takes credit for your work, a hypercritical parent, or an abusive partner who threatens violence if you cross him or her or try to leave. Wherever such toxic people show up, they create negativity in their relationships. Sometimes they are even dangerous.

Sadly for the9m—and for you—people who have been toxic for a while aren't likely to change. If you've been living with a parent, spouse, or significant other who puts you down, yells at you, manipulates you, or generally takes advantage of you, it probably won't get better. If you work for a narcissistic manager who always finds a way to keep you off balance, don't expect it to change. Toxic people always have a reason why they can't do better or feel better, and they have a gift for making it other people's fault. If we're around such people too much of the time, it can feel almost impossible to avoid sinking into a quicksand of hopelessness.

A toxic relationship is *not* better than none. It takes up time and emotional space. It's important to let these relationships go or to at least separate from them emotionally. But that's only half of the project. To have genuine self-esteem requires us to find the courage to forge healthy, positive relationships with people we can depend on and who depend on us.

Substance Abuse

Substance abuse is hostile to genuine self-esteem. If your best friend is a bottle, a pipe, or a pill, you can't have healthy relationships with other people. Don't kid yourself; you can't. You'll always be at the mercy of your need for another drink or the next smoke, pill, or whatever you're dependent on. The same holds true for hanging out with people who are substance abusers. Drinking and drugging buddies are unlikely to be able to maintain a mutually supportive, helping relationship. They may be great conversationalists when under the influence. They may be mellow fellows to hang with. But they're unlikely to have the energy or commitment to extend themselves if you want to do something other than use or if you need them.

> In high school, Ashley wasn't teased so much as ignored. "I felt like a ghost sometimes," she says. "I'd go from class to class, and no one seemed to notice I was there." One day while walking home from school, she ran into a few girls who were sharing a joint. They thought it would be funny to ask her to join them. *Why not?* she thought. Suddenly she found that she was part of a group. Her willingness to buy and share marijuana won her instant acceptance, something she hadn't had before. "By the end of the year, I was seriously drug dependent," Ashley says. "Once I tried weed, I figured why not try other stuff too?"
>
> She got a wake-up call one night when she woke up alone in the woods. Cold, shaking, and scared, she took a look around and realized that her "buddies" had left her there. "That's when I realized that some friends are worse than none." The happy ending to this story is that Ashley cleaned up her act, managed to graduate, and started taking classes at a community college in a nearby town. "Getting out of high school was the best thing for me," she says. "I needed a chance to start over. I found some people like me when I joined a service sorority. It wasn't easy and I know I have a ways to go, but I feel like I'm finally making some good decisions."

It's beyond the mission of this book to support someone to sobriety. If you can't get clean and sober on your own, look for a substance abuse program and counselor. And if you keep falling for alcoholics and addicts, please get yourself into therapy to figure out why you're drawn to people who are emotionally unavailable to you. Your genuine self-esteem depends on it.

Assessing How Connected You Are

The following self-assessment will give you a rough idea of how socially connected you are. Read through the statements below and check off all that are true of you.

_____ 1. I have at least one friend (other than a spouse or partner) who knows just about everything about me.

_____ 2. I'm friendly to anyone I see, such as shopkeepers, waitstaff, and crossing guards.

_____ 3. I have a network of caring people I can reach out to when I need support.

_____ 4. I do what I can to make my community a better place.

_____ 5. I have someone in my life (other than family members) whom I can call for support even at 3:00 a.m.

_____ 6. I regularly thank people who are helpful, such as grocery baggers, volunteers at my kids' schools, or people who hold a door for me.

_____ 7. My partner or spouse is one of my best friends.

_____ 8. When disaster strikes in my community, I look for ways to help others.

_____ 9. I have an older, wiser person in my network who's an important role model.

_____ 10. I regularly let people in my life know how much they mean to me.

_____ 11. I have several friends who regularly call me or see me.

_____ 12. I make it a point to do random acts of kindness for other people.

_____ 13. My friends on social media are mostly people I also have face time with.

_____ 14. When a friend needs me, I do my best to be helpful.

Even numbers are ways that you're doing good for others. Odd numbers indicate that you've built a community of support for yourself. The higher the number of each, the more likely you are to be happy and healthy.

Activity Choices for Creating and Caring for Relationships

Throughout his career, psychologist Alfred Adler maintained that there are three fundamental tasks of life that we each must master if we are to be happy and mentally healthy: we need to find meaningful work, create a circle of friends, and find an intimate other with whom to share our lives. All three tasks are based in relationships. Being connected isn't an extra. Getting and staying connected is fundamental to health, happiness, and genuine self-esteem. The following activities can all help you maintain and strengthen your connections.

Improve Your Social Skills

Lately, I've been seeing an ad on TV featuring a teenage boy who isn't at all a stereotypical heart-throb talking about how he's "the man" in his high school. Why? Because he's watched chick flicks (courtesy of the cable package he's hawking) and learned all the tricks for dating teenage girls. The ad ends with him walking down the hall arm in arm with a cheerleader.

Okay, it's corny. But there's a lesson in it. Even if you think you don't have social skills, and the need to make small talk leaves you tongue-tied and awkward, there are ways to improve. Make doing so a personal project. Pick up a few self-help books (or watch some chick flicks!), gather up your courage, practice in front of a mirror, and act "as if" (as described in chapter 4, on courage). Get some therapy if you need it. Do whatever you need to do to feel more comfortable interacting with other people. You don't need to be the life of the party. You just need to be able to engage in a little conversation—maybe with another shy person who looks like he or she would like to be somewhere else. Remember, we're born to be social!

Practice Social Graces

Have you noticed? If you let another car go ahead of you in traffic, the driver often gives a little wave. It may only be a raise of a couple of fingers, or it may be a full-on wave, but few people skip it altogether. That little wave is a social convention that makes us more likely to be courteous again. Why? Let's look at the sequence: You let someone go ahead. The person waves. You smile. Yielding is such a little thing, yet it can lead to feeling, however briefly, that we've made a friendly connection. We've done good, and we feel good for having done so.

Social graces also include what I call courtesy language: "hello," "good-bye," "please," "thank you," and "excuse me." Those words ease our way whether we are in our neighborhood, on a crowded bus, or traveling in a country where we don't speak the language. They are the basic phrases of consideration for others. I imagine you notice it, probably not happily, when people fail to use those simple words. Being polite is an important part of what greases the wheels of the social world. It doesn't cost a penny or take extra time to be polite to the people we encounter throughout our day. It's such a simple way of doing good. When we do, we make the world a little friendlier and kinder.

One day I was chatting with a young mom while sharing a playground bench. I was shocked when she told me she wasn't going to teach her kids to be polite. "It's so phony," she said. "Why should they have to pony up a 'please' to get something I'm going to give them anyway? And why should they be thanking everyone who just does what they're supposed to do?"

Sometimes it really *is* hard to be polite. I wanted to give her my best lecture on why she was doing her kids a great disservice. But I learned long ago that uninvited advice usually isn't well-received. If she had asked me, I would have said, in the politest way possible, of course, that her kids would probably be seen as quite obnoxious by the rest of the world. Simple expressions of gratitude ("please" and "thank you") and acknowledgment of times when we may have bumped others or gotten in their way ("excuse me") are part of what helps people get along. It's not phony. It's a sincere way to acknowledge others and connect positively.

Take Time for Friend Maintenance

You probably wouldn't neglect maintaining your car on schedule. Why should your friends deserve any less consideration? Like a car, friendships need regular tune-ups to keep humming along. Without regular contact, friendships tend to fade away. If you're not in touch for six months, it will take some effort to reconnect.

As with any new habit, developing a practice of maintaining friendships takes time, commitment, and practice. Below, you'll find a nice clean calendar for the next month of your life. (For a downloadable version of the calendar, visit http://www.newharbinger.com/31021; see the back of the book for information on how to access it.) Add the dates, then write in any social activities and contacts you've already scheduled or that you do regularly. Going to work doesn't count, but if you go out to lunch with a coworker you like, it does. If you aren't spending quality time with people you care about at least a few times a month, or at least making contact by phone or e-mail, you're sorely neglecting your friends. You're also reducing your sense of community and your own genuine self-esteem.

Do remember the "quality" in quality time. Talking about the weather, the latest episode of *The Bachelor*, or how your favorite sports team is doing is better than nothing. But to increase your genuine self-esteem, you also need to ask how others are and care enough to listen to the answer. You need to be there to celebrate them as well as offer comfort. And you need to be willing to let them be a friend to you by celebrating and comforting you as well.

If that calendar is just about blank, make a plan to do more friend maintenance. Here are a few suggestions on activities you might add:

- Note days when you can take a few minutes to phone a friend, just to touch base and see how your friend is doing.

- Make a couple of coffee dates.

- Commit to sending a card, note, or e-mail to a friend or acquaintance at least once a week.

- Invite someone to go to a game, concert, or exhibit. Plan on spending a little time before or after the event to really talk—and not just about the event.

- Accept invitations that come your way. If none are forthcoming, let folks know you're available.

Repeat this activity each month until getting in touch and spending quality time with friends is a habit.

> Mable, who's in her seventies, is great at friend maintenance. In addition to making the usual spontaneous phone calls, sending birthday cards, and so on, she keeps a list of her closest friends and their addresses and phone numbers on her desk. Every day, she writes or calls one of them and checks that person off. When she gets to the end of the list, she starts over again. Not trusting herself to mentally keep track, she's come up with this system to be sure that the people she cares about know that she's thinking of them.
>
> What goes around comes around. When Mable had a stroke, those people were immediately there for her. Of course, that wasn't why she had kept up her friendships. She did it because, in her words, "it's how you love the people you love." By staying in touch, Mable and her circle of friends provide a network of caring and support for one another in both bad times and good.

Month _____

Sunday	Monday	Tuesday	Wednesday	Thursday	Friday	Saturday

Deepen Your Friendships

To feel connected, it's crucial that we really, truly know at least a few friends in the inner Dunbar circle discussed earlier in this chapter. That means more than spending time together. It means sharing our hopes, fears, dreams, and worries. It means letting them know they're important to us and accepting their support when we need it. Such relationships increase our genuine self-esteem. Both people feel honored to be brought closer and feel happier in the knowledge that they've got a real friend.

Here's an exercise that can help you deepen your friendships. (For a downloadable worksheet, visit http://www.newharbinger.com/31021.) Begin by thinking of up to three people whom you consider to be your closest friends.

Name of friend: _____

What I most admire about this person: _____

_____

Why I'm glad this person is in my life: _____

_____

Something I'm willing to share about myself to get closer: _____

_____

Name of friend: _____

What I most admire about this person: _____

_____

Why I'm glad this person is in my life: _____

_____

Something I'm willing to share about myself to get closer: _____

_____

Name of friend: _____

What I most admire about this person: _____

_____

Why I'm glad this person is in my life: _____

_____

Something I'm willing to share about myself to get closer: _____

_____

You get the idea. Do the same for everyone in your life you'd like to know better. Then make a plan to take your relationship with each person to the next level. One possibility is to do a gratitude visit, as described in chapter 5, for each person on your list.

Reach Out and Touch Someone

People need physical contact. To cite only a couple of examples of current research, one study found that soothing behaviors between adults promote enhanced health and well-being (Coan, Schaefer, and Davidson 2006). All babies thrive on touch, but preemies need it even more. Indeed, researchers have found that premature babies gain needed weight when they get regular, moderate massages (Field, Diego, and Hernandez-Reif 2001).

Think about how to increase physical contact in your life. Keep it safe. Only touch those who are close enough to you to invite and appreciate the touching. Full-body hugs are nice, but not necessary. A stroke on the arm, a touch of the hand when talking, a quick rub of someone's shoulder—all can enhance your relationships and increase your genuine self-esteem.

Reflect on whether there is enough touch in your life. If not, are there ways for you to increase the frequency and variety of safe touch with those in your innermost Dunbar circle? List your ideas here:

_____

_____

_____

_____

_____

Volunteer

If you're alone and lonely, it's unlikely that someone is going to knock on your door to fix it. You have to do something. If your friend census is down, an effective way to meet people is to volunteer. Every community has organizations that need help. Nonprofit organizations often need people to staff the phones and help with events. Hospitals often need volunteers to work in a gift shop, give attention to sick babies, or staff an information desk. By getting involved in something that interests you, you'll meet new people who share those interests. Some may even become friends. Even if they don't, you'll feel better because you're doing something that matters. Volunteering need not take a lot of your time—unless you have a lot of time you want to give. Just a few hours a week can make a huge difference to someone in need and give a big boost to your genuine self-esteem.

> My client Dawn, a woman in her thirties, lived alone and worked as a personal care attendant for a disabled woman. Both of Dawn's best friends had moved in the past year, and she'd been feeling increasingly depressed. They kept in touch by Skype, but Dawn knew she also needed local friends to do things with. She hadn't made new friends in years and wasn't sure she knew how. So during our next session, I pulled out the page from our local paper that listed volunteer opportunities. There, Dawn found a listing for a group that helps the spouses of international graduate students get acquainted with our town. She thought that might be fun.
>
> When she came in a couple of weeks later, I saw a new Dawn. She had met with members of the group who were involved with planning activities. As a lifelong resident in our town, she'd been able to contribute ideas that were welcomed. Best of all, she thought several of the women she'd met had friend potential. After a few months, she was happily involved with new friendships and renewed interests. Our work was done. Remember PERMA? Dawn was feeling *positive*, was *engaged* in a project that had *meaning* for her, had developed new *relationships*, and was experiencing feelings of *achievement* in making things happen. By doing good, she was feeling much better.

Do Gratitude

There's an all-too-human tendency to take the people in our lives for granted. Acknowledging the ways that others enhance your life is a way to both do good and feel good. Perhaps not surprisingly, Barbara Fredrickson and her colleagues found that if you're a happy person, you're more likely to recognize kindness and be kind. They didn't expect to also find that the act of being grateful makes us be more kind (2009). There's one catch: acts of gratitude must be genuine and from the heart. Phony gratitude rings false because it is false. Don't ever let it become routine or perfunctory. If need be, take a moment to feel gratitude before doing it.

You may wonder how to *do* gratitude. Here are a few ideas to help you think about ways you might get started:

- Simply say thank you when you wouldn't normally do so. A heartfelt thank-you to the kid who bags your groceries can make his or her day.

- Keep a stack of thank-you cards on your desk. Spend five minutes of your work day thinking about who has done something for you. Then write a brief note of thanks and send it.

- Post a message of gratitude on a friend's Facebook page.

- Invite a coworker who's helped you to lunch—your treat.

- Put notes of love and gratitude in your loved ones' lunch bags or under their pillows.

- Call someone to say thank you or leave a thank-you message on his or her voicemail.

Now think about acts of gratitude that appeal to you and that fit your values. Add them to the list. Then commit to doing a few of them over the course of the next week.

1._____

2._____

3._____

4._____

5._____

Doing gratitude makes the world a kinder, gentler place. It increases our positivity and helps us feel good about life.

At the wake for a friend, I was struck by what her daughters shared. They spoke eloquently of their mother's support and love. She had regularly put notes of encouragement and appreciation in their lunch boxes when they were little. When they went out of their way to do something kind, they got a special hug. She thanked them when they did their chores and let them know how much she appreciated having such kind and lovely girls for daughters. No, it wasn't over-the-top mushy. Her daughters also heard about it when they'd done something wrong. However, their mom had quietly, steadily provided an environment of gratitude in their home, for which they remained very grateful.

Go on a Gratitude Visit

The gratitude visit has become such an integral exercise in positive psychology that it's hard to know who to credit. Martin Seligman talks about it in *Flourish* (2011), but I remember doing something much like it in human potential workshops in the 1970s. It springs from the reality that we often don't think to stop and thank the people who have had positive impact on our lives. Most of us have had moments where a coach, teacher, relative, or friend has done or said just the right thing when we needed it. Sometimes such moments send us in a new direction or give us the encouragement we need to take on a problem or meet the next challenge. A basic strategy for increasing your positivity is to tell other people that you're thankful for them. Here's how a gratitude visit works:

1. Think of a person you feel gratitude toward for something he or she did in the past.

2. Write a letter to that person describing what he or she did and how it made your life richer or better in some way.

3. Contact the person and arrange to meet face-to-face if you can. If you can't, phone contact is fine. Read your letter to the person.

You may be surprised to find how much your acknowledgment means to the person. You may also be surprised at how much it contributes to your sense of genuine self-esteem.

Who would you write to? _____

Write your gratitude letter here or, if you need more space, write or type it on a separate piece of paper.

Date: _____

Dear _____,

_____

_____

_____

_____

_____

_____

_____

_____

After your visit, take some time to sit with your thoughts and feelings. Then record your reactions here while they're still fresh:

_____

_____

_____

_____

_____

You can also do a virtual version of this exercise, which is useful when it's not possible to get in touch with the person you'd like to thank. Relationships don't end with death or distance. They live on in our hearts and in our memories. In such cases, write your letter anyway. Then sit opposite an empty chair and imagine the person sitting across from you. Really take the time to imagine the experience of being with the person. Then read your letter out loud. Stay quiet for a time afterward and let yourself sit with your feelings.

Record your reactions here while they're still fresh:

_____

_____

_____

_____

_____

Write a Letter Asking for Forgiveness

Being human, you've probably done and said hurtful things. We all make mistakes. Decency requires that we feel bad about them, especially if they've hurt other people. Psychologist Kristin Neff's work on self-compassion (2011) highlights the importance of forgiving ourselves if we are to be true to positive values and maintain positive relationships. The purpose of this activity is to help you stop beating yourself up over something you did in the past and start to resolve your guilt and shame. By actively asking for forgiveness, you may be able to repair a relationship. By acknowledging your own contribution to a problem, you do something worthy and can feel better about yourself.

Think of someone you feel you've wronged in the past: _____

What did you do that you now regret?

_____

_____

_____

Did it seem like it made sense at the time? If so, why?

_____

_____

_____

What's your understanding of your actions now that time has passed and you've thought about it?

_____

_____

_____

Now take a moment to think deeply about the situation. Give yourself the same understanding and compassion you'd extend to a good friend who did something hurtful and now feels terrible about it. Find a way to forgive yourself for being human and doing something you now regret.

Next, write a letter to the person, acknowledging what you did and how guilty and ashamed you've felt about it. Express your remorse and apologize. If you need more space, write or type your letter on a separate piece of paper.

Date: _____

Dear _____,

_____

_____

_____

_____

_____

_____

_____

_____

Sending the letter is optional. If you think it might be well-received and you want to heal the relationship, you might send it to see how the other person will respond. The worst that may happen is that the person doesn't forgive you, leaving you in the same position. It's possible, though, that the two of you can agree to make a new start. On the other hand, sometimes reopening a hurtful event only makes things worse. If the other person has moved on, it might be wiser and kinder to both of you to leave things be.

Record your reactions to this activity while they're still fresh.

_____

_____

_____

_____

_____

Let Go of Toxic Connections

As we discussed in chapter 5, on positivity, there are times when forgiveness and positive thinking simply aren't a good idea. Giving an abusive partner the ninety-ninth chance to be good to you, living with a parent who constantly puts you down and thinks it's only what you deserve, hanging out with people who only let you in the group if you accept being the brunt of put-downs or join in their unhealthy lifestyle—these aren't healthy or positive ways to live. In such situations, get out as best you can as soon as you can.

Yes, I know. It can be hard to leave. Sometimes it's impossible. If you're young, you may be dependent on toxic family members for the roof over your head and food to eat. If you're in a toxic partnership, you may have been manipulated into a dependent position and find yourself with no money, no friends, and no self-confidence. If so, you're not alone—and you're also not alone in having difficulty getting free. Women often leave an abusive relationship multiple times before they leave for good. If this sounds like you, contact a domestic violence program and get some help. For support, you can call the National Domestic Violence Hotline at their toll-free number: 1-800-799-7233. Counselors are available 24/7. Do be careful. Toxic people don't like to be crossed. If you think your abuser might access your computer or phone, use someone else's to contact people who can help you.

Even if you can't leave a toxic relationship physically, you can leave emotionally. Toxic people only have power over your mind and heart if you let them. You don't have to believe what they say or accept their judgments. You may have to pretend to go along while you plot your escape, but you can still hold on to your own sense of self until you get out. In the meanwhile, work on developing your genuine self-esteem to rediscover and develop the skills you need to take care of yourself.

All of that said, remember that toxic people can range from those who are truly abusive to those who are just unpleasant. If there are people in your life who are toxic to your genuine self-esteem, write their names here. If you worry that any of them might find this book, just mentally note their names.

_____

_____

_____

_____

Rituals have power. It's why people burn old love letters, tear up pictures to literally tear someone out of their life, or light a candle to seal a vow. You may not be able to separate from toxic people right away, but you can create a ritual that will help you let go of their negative effects on you. Because rituals are highly personal, I'll leave it to you to create your own. Most importantly, for the sake of your genuine self-esteem, refuse to let toxic people's opinions of you poison your opinion of yourself. Meditate on it. Let go of their toxicity in your life.

Find Positive Friends

Once you let go of the toxic people in your life, there's more room for cultivating positive relationships, whether with new friends or a new romantic partner. Positive people are compassionate, supportive, and helpful. They want the best for us and give us openhearted love and care. They are the very opposite of toxic. They are people who have genuine self-esteem and plenty of it.

Think about the people in your life who are already positive members of your social circle. Consider giving them a Gratitude Visit as described in chapter 5, to let them know how much you appreciate them. If you don't yet have such friends, think about people you admire who you wish could be there for you. Think about their qualities and what they contribute to their community. If there isn't a way you can get to know those specific people, consider searching for people with similar qualities. Chances are, they're not going to just show up in your life. You have to be willing to look. That may mean joining a group or starting to take part in community activities. Show up. Show up regularly and contribute what you can. People with genuine self-esteem generally do find each other.

Be Part of Your Community

A big circle of friends isn't required to be social. Not everyone is an extrovert. Not everyone can juggle five best friends. One or two people in your inner circle may be enough for you. But we can all be more connected. Feeling part of our community is an important aspect of feeling comfortable and at home. It doesn't take a lot of effort to learn the name of the kid who delivers the newspaper or to introduce yourself to a salesclerk you see regularly. It's painless to say hello to a neighbor who's passing by. If you go to the same coffee shop nearly every day, you become a familiar face. Over time, people will start to recognize you and say hello. It feels great to be acknowledged with a smile. The more of these little incidental connections you make, the more you'll feel that you have a place in the social fabric of your community and the more your genuine self-esteem will grow.

Brainstorm a list of places in your community where people congregate who are likely to share your values and interests, such as a special coffee shop, a local pub, a hobby shop, the library, a park, a gym, or a yoga class.

_____

_____

_____

Now do whatever it takes to become a regular at one or more of those places for a while. It may be uncomfortable at first. Smile. Exchange pleasant remarks and be friendly. If you connect with others, they will connect with you. That's what being part of a community is all about.

Caley is a very private person who enjoys living alone. She has one really good friend from work who she occasionally does things with and another old friend from high school who stays in touch with a phone call now and then. But Caley isn't lonely or isolated; she's deeply embedded in her community. She has attended the same church for years and has a passing acquaintance with other members. Every weekday morning she gets her coffee at the same drive-up window and says a cheery hello to the same server. When she goes to the library, the person at the front desk greets her with a smile and says, "How are you today?" She and her rescue greyhound go to greyhound events, where she compares notes and shares pleasantries with other owners of those magnificent dogs. She has a strong sense of community—on her own terms.

Finding Love

How to find a special person to love is beyond the scope of this book. But many of the same strategies already talked about in this chapter apply. People who become close friends first are the most promising people to become lovers. People who share your values, who feel good about themselves, and who do good for others are the folks who are most likely to cherish you and who you will most want to spend your life with. Don't waste your time on anything less. You deserve a relationship with someone who has genuine self-esteem.

Remember What This Is All About

Remember, genuine self-esteem has two parts that reinforce and support each other. To live comfortably in quadrant 3, we need to do good and worthy things so we can feel good and hold ourselves in high self-regard. The recipients of the good things we do are other people. By letting go of toxic people and by forming and maintaining positive relationships, we can enhance our genuine self-esteem. We can deepen our personal connections and become more integrated into our larger human community.

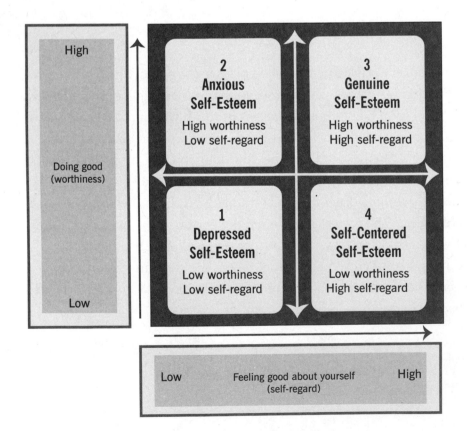

CHAPTER 8

Make a Plan

Find a happy person, and you will find a project.

—Sonja Lyubomirsky

Having genuine self-esteem means both feeling good about yourself (believing in your own self-worth) and doing good, worthwhile things in the world—things that are consistent with your values system—in order to earn those good feelings. This book has outlined the following keys for increasing and strengthening your genuine self-esteem:

- Identifying and living your values

- Paying attention to self-care

- Developing courage

- Embracing positivity

- Practicing mindfulness

- Cultivating positive relationships

Thinking about all of these keys is a start. But the whole point of the two-part definition of self-esteem is that it requires action. We have to act on our good intentions and positive values to attain the self-confidence and connections we want and need to live a richer, happier life.

Nine Steps to Unlocking the Secrets of Genuine Self-Esteem

If you've been completing the activities in chapters 4 through 7, you're already on the road to becoming more self-confident and connected. If not, or if your engagement with the activities has been hit or miss, this chapter will help you draw up a systematic plan for making changes. Doing so can be more powerful than you may realize. In fact, research shows that even just having goals makes people happier (Lyubomirsky 2008). Setting goals will help you focus your efforts.

In this chapter, I'll outline a process for making changes. At the end of the chapter, you'll find a few examples of how this approach has worked for others.

1. **Make sure self-esteem is your problem.** Take another look at the self-esteem grid in chapter 1. The goal is to live in quadrant 3 most of the time. If that isn't the case for you, you may indeed be in a crisis of self-esteem.

2. **Take time for physical preparation.** You need to take care of yourself if you are to feel good and to have the energy to work on your self-esteem.

3. **Remind yourself of your core values and character strengths.** Review your work in chapter 2. If you haven't done so already, visit http://www.authentichappiness .sas.upenn.edu to identify your character strengths. Basing your decisions on a strong values system is central to genuine self-esteem.

4. **Do a careful self-analysis by reviewing the informal assessments in chapters 4 through 7.** In order to get where you want to go, you need to know where you are. When creating an action plan, you'll want to target areas that could use improvement.

5. **Make a three-month plan.** The overarching goal is to increase your genuine self-esteem. That can feel like a tall order. It's wise to set subgoals that are small and attainable within a short amount of time. I therefore suggest that you start with a three-month plan of action.

6. **Commit to your plan.** Really commit. Three months isn't a long time, but it is a realistic time frame in which to reduce old habits and establish new patterns. You owe yourself at least that amount of time to change your life.

7. **Keep a journal of your progress.** Start a diary, scrapbook, sketchbook, or computer document. Keeping a record of your journey will help provide daily motivation. Looking back over your progress will inspire you when you feel discouraged.

8. **Be accountable.** Most people stick to a program better when they're accountable to other people. Enlist a buddy. Start a blog. Post updates on Facebook. Join an online support group. If you need professional support, consider working with a therapist to help you stay on track. Having people celebrate your successes and encourage you when you're in a slump will help you stay on your path.

9. **Always be willing to adjust and repeat.** The plan you'll create in this chapter is *your* plan for *your* life. If something isn't working, change the plan. If you really like what happens when you try one of the activities, do it again. If you're happy with your results at the three-month mark, consider re-upping. Better yet, think about ways you can fully integrate the doing part of genuine self-esteem into a lifelong habit.

One important note: Making and following a self-help plan isn't therapy, although it can be very therapeutic. Your work with this book is a good example of life coaching, not therapy. If you give it a good try and still feel down on yourself, depressed, or anxious and unsure that you can change your situation, please consider making an appointment with a mental health professional for an evaluation. Sometimes trying to understand your own motivations or see your own stumbling blocks is like trying to see your own face without the benefit of a mirror. A therapist can offer you new perspectives on your thoughts and behaviors and provide you with emotional support and practical suggestions to facilitate change.

Finally, as a reminder, I've also compiled a list of recommended readings and Internet-based talks and animations that you might find helpful in your journey. This list of companion resources is available for download at http://www.newharbinger.com/31021. (See the back of the book for instructions on how to access the file.)

Three Months to More Genuine Self-Esteem

Now it's time for you to draft your own plan for increasing your genuine self-esteem. Here's a blank form for you to use. (For a downloadable version, visit http://www.newharbinger.com/31021.)

1. **Is self-esteem your problem?** _____ yes _____ no

Did you rule out medical and medication problems? _____ yes _____ no

If not, make sure you aren't ignoring an undiagnosed or undertreated physical problem or side effects from medications.

Where do you live most of the time—in which quadrant of the self-esteem grid? _____

Remember, as discussed in chapter 1, genuine self-esteem is in quadrant 3. Many people visit the other quadrants in both healthy and unhealthy ways some of the time. If this is true for you, take a moment to reflect on those visits. Make a few notes here about elements of your life that you are okay about leaving in quadrant 1, 2, or 4:

_____

_____

_____

_____

Make some notes about any issues that need to be resolved so that you can move to living more fully in quadrant 3:

_____

_____

_____

_____

2. **Take time for physical preparation.** If you haven't yet worked through chapter 3 (Self-Care and Getting Ready for Change) in detail, please do so before continuing.

If there are changes you need to make to be at your best, make some notes about them here:

_____

_____

_____

_____

_____

3.   Remind yourself of your core values and character strengths. Start by listing your five character strengths:

1. _____

2. _____

3. _____

4. _____

5. _____

If you have other values that aren't adequately expressed by your character strengths, list them here:

_____

_____

_____

_____

_____

List any strengths and values that you'd like to emphasize more in your daily life:

_____

_____

_____

4.   Do a careful self-analysis by reviewing the informal assessments in chapters 4 through 7. In what order do you need to attend to the areas covered in those chapters? I recommend starting with the easiest and going from there. However, if self-care is a problem, that's probably the best place to start. Number the areas below from 1 to 5, with 1 being the area you want to tackle first.

_____   Self-care

_____ Courage

_____ Positivity

_____ Mindfulness

_____ Relationships

5. Make a three-month plan. For each month, choose one or two key areas to work on: self-care, courage, positivity, mindfulness, or relationships. Then choose two or three activities to help you achieve your monthly goal. (Lists of all of the activities in chapters 4 through 7 appear below to help you with this step.) None of the activities is better than others. If you like a particular activity, do it a number of times. Feel free to add your own ideas. The important thing is to identify strategies that work for you.

Month 1 goal: _____

Activities to work on that goal:

1. _____

2. _____

3. _____

Month 2 goal: _____

Activities to work on that goal:

1. _____

2. _____

3. _____

Month 3 goal: _____

Activities to work on that goal:

1. _____

2. _____

3. _____

6. Commit to your plan. If you didn't do so already, go back to the contract at the end of chapter 3 and sign it. Commit to making the changes you need to make to be a healthier, happier you.

7. Keep a journal of your progress. Make journaling a daily ritual to track your progress and also your setbacks. What will you do to make sure you keep track of your program?

_____

_____

8. Be accountable. Who can you enlist to support you? You're more likely to stick with your plan if you have a buddy or if you check in regularly with someone who cares.

_____

_____

_____

9. Always be willing to adjust and repeat.

Activity Choices

The following lists of all of the activities in this book may feel like one of those menus that have far too many choices. Don't let yourself get overwhelmed. Remember, you don't need to do all of them any more than you need to order everything on the menu for your dinner. Go with your gut. You don't want to get so immobilized by choosing that you never get to actually doing. Check off those that are appealing to you, then make a commitment to the doing. Do something this week that will get you closer to your goals.

Courage (chapter 4)

_____   Give Yourself Credit for the Courage You Have

_____   Write a New Script

_____   Learn How to Learn from Mistakes

_____   Practice Making Mistakes

_____   Call in Reinforcements

_____   Act "As If"

_____ Make What Goes Around Come Around

_____ Get Physical

_____ Take a Stand by Standing Up

_____ Take a Stand by Writing

Positivity (chapter 5)

_____ Identify Your Character Strengths

_____ Use Your Character Strengths

_____ Engage with Problems

_____ Count the Good Stuff

_____ Keep Things in Perspective

_____ Reframe the Bad Stuff

_____ Do Random Acts of Kindness

_____ Make a Bragging Box

_____ Pay It Forward

_____ Thank Yourself

_____ Write a Letter Forgiving Someone

Mindfulness (chapter 6)

_____ Experience RAIN

_____ Follow the Breath

_____ Use Guided Meditations

_____ Use a Mantra

_____ Tune In to What Already Is

_____ Imagine Your Happy Place

_____ Practice Walking Meditation

_____ Eat Mindfully

_____ Listen to Music Mindfully

_____ Make Friends with Your Hand

Relationships (chapter 7)

_____ Improve Your Social Skills

_____ Practice Social Graces

_____ Take Time for Friend Maintenance

_____ Deepen Your Friendships

_____ Reach Out and Touch Someone

_____ Volunteer

_____ Do Gratitude

_____ Go on a Gratitude Visit

_____ Write a Letter Asking for Forgiveness

_____ Let Go of Toxic Connections

_____ Find Positive Friends

_____ Be Part of Your Community

Twofers

Some of the activities can both increase your positivity and enhance relationships:

_____ Do Random Acts of Kindness

_____ Pay It Forward

_____ Do Gratitude

_____ Go on a Gratitude Visit

_____ Write a Letter Forgiving Someone

_____ Write a Letter Asking for Forgiveness

Case Histories

Sometimes it's helpful to see how others have integrated a new idea into their life. I've included short summaries of three sample plans here—not to suggest that these plans would be appropriate for you, but rather to help you see how individuals at different stages of life went about increasing their genuine self-esteem. (In order to protect the privacy of people who were kind enough to try out the activities while this book was in development, I've created fictionalized composite characters.) Whether you're a young adult, in midlife, or older, you can take charge of your life in a new way to develop or enhance your genuine self-esteem.

Dakota: A Quarter-Life Crisis Averted

Dakota is twenty-five. "I think I'm in a quarter-life crisis," she said. "I'm in a job I like well enough, but it's going nowhere. I don't have much in common with friends who are getting married and having kids, so we don't see each other much anymore. I'm not sure my boyfriend is the right one for me. It's comfortable and all, but he doesn't like to do much besides hang out. I guess I think if I liked myself more, maybe I'd have the guts to make some changes. I don't want to find myself in the same spot five years from now."

Like many Millennials, she'd had lots of love and support from her folks. Smart and smiley, she generally did better than average in school and got along with people. She said, "My parents never pressured me much. They just wanted me to go to get the education I needed to land a decent job." That gave her the freedom to explore her interests in art and design. She valued having a wide circle of friends and feeling creative and energized by group projects. Although she had a well-paying job in an advertising firm, she was in a cubicle all day doing administrative work. There was little opportunity for creativity or social interaction. She agreed that neither her home life nor her work life currently reflected her values. Her background supported genuine self-esteem, but her current situation didn't. She didn't feel very good about herself, and she wasn't doing things that made her feel like her life was going in a worthwhile direction. She was spending far too much time in quadrant 1: depressed self-esteem, with a low sense of worthiness and low self-regard.

We started at the beginning, with self-care. Dakota thought she was doing okay in that department. She went to the gym three evenings a week and tried to eat healthfully. Sometimes she skimped on sleep, but she slept in on weekends. She didn't see it as a problem that she and her boyfriend tended to drink a lot when they went out. That worried me more than it did her, but she wasn't open to talking about it yet.

Having had things come easily to her most of her life, Dakota didn't know how to assert herself and take the risks necessary to go for things she wanted. She was excited about where she was working, but she wasn't a bit excited about what she was actually doing. Similarly, she was afraid to break up with her boyfriend because she wasn't sure she'd find someone who would better meet her needs. "The good ones are already committed," she said. She didn't have the social circle she was used to. We needed to help her find the courage and positivity to get active in creating the life she really wanted instead of settling for what had evolved.

Dakota developed the following three-month plan for herself to help her utilize her strengths, widen her social circle, and look more carefully at her relationship.

Dakota's Plan

Character strengths: *sociability, optimism, humor, creativity, curiosity*

Values: *My character strengths pretty much sum up my values.*

Month 1 goal: *Increase positivity.*

Activities to work on that goal:

1. *Engage with Problems*

2. *Use Your Character Strengths*

3. *Make a Bragging Box*

Month 2 goal: *Increase courage.*

Activities to work on that goal:

1. *Give Yourself Credit for the Courage You Have*

2. *Practice Making Mistakes*

3. *Act "As If"*

Month 3 goal: *Work on mindfulness.*

Activities to work on that goal:

1. *Learn to meditate*

Note that Dakota only chose one activity for the third month. This was fine. She wanted to leave room for adjusting or changing her plan in response to whatever happened in months 1 and 2. Besides, to her, learning to meditate looked like a big deal.

What Happened

Dakota showed great commitment to her plan over the next three months. Here are some notes on her experience.

Month 1: Increasing Positivity

Engage with Problems: Organizing and filing wasn't at all what Dakota had in mind when she accepted her job. She was alone much of the time, and her job didn't let her use her creativity. With some support from me, she was able to engage with the problem and find the courage to ask her supervisor to explore some options. He was willing to put her on a special project to see whether she had the skills to branch into the creative department. It was a good start. Working on the project helped her feel less isolated, and she was able to investigate whether the creative end of the work was really what she wanted.

Use Your Character Strengths: We brainstormed ways for Dakota to align her free time with her character strengths of curiosity and creativity. She decided to take a weekly art class and be more assertive with her boyfriend about doing things, like going to art exhibits, that were fun and satisfying for her. His reluctance to even give it a try provided more evidence that maybe he wasn't the guy for her. Also, instead of being upset that her friends with children couldn't go out, she started joining in when they were walking their babies or monitoring the playground. She found they still had lots to talk about.

Make a Bragging Box: Dakota needed to have more evidence of ways she'd already been creative in order to gather the courage to pursue some of her dreams. With a nudge from me, she brought in some items to get started: a sketch she had done for a college art class that she really liked; a photo of her apartment, which she had decorated both cheaply and creatively; and a scarf she loves. Prior to making the box, she hadn't fully reaffirmed that the things she was most proud of had to do with visual art.

Month 2: Increasing Courage

Give Yourself Credit for the Courage You Have: Dakota tended to underestimate the courage she already had. In high school, she had painted her bedroom an extremely bright shade of yellow-green. (It worked!) She enjoyed putting together offbeat and artsy outfits. She hadn't married her boyfriend, a guy who was comfortable but not quite right. She draws the line when some of her friends tell racist jokes. Recognizing and claiming the many ways she's already courageous gave her self-confidence a boost.

Practice Making Mistakes: Dakota's fear of taking risks was rooted in a fear of making mistakes. We talked about how to keep things in perspective in order to reduce her anxiety. She then agreed to make a game of making at least one "mistake" a day to test out her admittedly irrational conviction that the world would then end. She wore two different color shoes to work one day. She "forgot" to turn in her timesheet on time. She wished her sister happy birthday on the wrong day. The world didn't end. Embarrassment didn't kill her. She found that other people didn't make a big deal of it, especially if she apologized, corrected the error, or, sometimes, laughed at herself.

Act "As If": Dakota realized she really did want to be a creative director. She gave a lot of thought to how the creative group at her firm worked. She realized they were all willing to contribute their ideas without taking it personally if someone else's was chosen by the client. By doing some role-plays, both with me and by herself, she practiced being less invested in approval and more willing to experiment.

Month 3: Working on Mindfulness

Learn to meditate: Dakota decided that meditation could wait. I hope she'll change her mind, as I do think it will help her be more relaxed and less anxious about her future. But when we reached the third month, Dakota wanted to keep up her momentum on working to transform her career into something that would be meaningful for her.

Dakota's Conclusions

After three months, Dakota was already feeling much better. Everything she had done so far was getting her out of an uncomfortable rut and into something more compelling. "I'm feeling more alive," she said. By giving herself permission to demonstrate her creativity and curiosity, she was getting more recognition at work. By deciding to meet old friends in ways that were comfortable for them, she revived some important relationships. The question of what to do about her relationship was still brewing, but she wanted to give it a little more time before making a decision. Her boyfriend was a nice guy. She did love him. She wanted to see if she had been blaming him when instead maybe she needed to change herself. That decision is yet another indication that she's now living with more genuine self-esteem.

Ella: Making Room for Her Better Self

At thirty-five years old, Ella was a successful interior designer and a single mom of two girls, ages eight and ten. She was constantly on the run, working to excel at her job and at being a mom. Over the last year, she'd been feeling less energetic, more irritable, and generally more negative. She felt guilty that she'd been increasingly short-tempered with her girls. She was resentful that she wasn't always recognized at work for being a top producer. She didn't feel good—or good about herself. She hated to admit it, but she was living far too much of her life in quadrant 2: anxious self-esteem, with a high sense of worthiness but low self-regard. She was constantly comparing herself to other moms and other designers and worried that she wasn't succeeding in either role.

Ella wasn't yet willing to look at making changes at home or work, so we agreed that self-care was the best place to start. She hadn't gone for a medical checkup for over four years. She'd stopped going to the gym months ago to save money, and she was often skimping on sleep so she could attend to work projects without taking time away from her daughters in the evenings.

On the other hand, she also had to admit that after putting the girls to bed she often plopped on the couch and mindlessly watched TV instead of using the next couple of hours well. That meant she had to stay up even later to get ready for the next day.

After looking into her values, Ella realized that she had been neglecting her health, despite it being important to her. And much to her dismay, she realized she'd been so caught up in all the things she thought she had to do that her girls had been getting a crabby, stressed-out mom instead of the warm, energetic mom Ella wanted to be.

When we looked over the other keys to genuine self-esteem, Ella decided she had more than enough courage and confidence, but that she'd been feeling negative about her life. Her relationship with her coworkers was prickly at best. Her connection to her daughters was too stressed. Developing more positivity was appealing. She also thought that starting to meditate would help her de-stress in a healthier way than watching late-night TV.

Taking all that information into account, Ella drew up the following plan.

Ella's Plan

Character strengths: *fairness, responsibility, creativity, enthusiasm, leadership*

Values: *Family first. I want to be sure that taking care of myself doesn't get in the way of giving my girls the positive attention they need. I also want to continue to give my job my all.*

Month 1 goal: *Take better care of myself.*

Activities to work on that goal:

1. *Get a checkup*

2. *Get more sleep*

3. *Build exercise into each day*

Month 2 goal: *Increase positivity.*

Activities to work on that goal:

1. *Count the Good Stuff—and keep a journal of it*

2. *Do Random Acts of Kindness*

3. *Do family maintenance*

Month 3 goal: *Be more mindful.*

Activities to work on that goal:

1. *Start meditating every day*

What Happened

At the end of the three months, Ella and I met again. Here's a summary of what she had to say about each element of her plan.

Month 1: Taking Better Care of Herself

Get a checkup: This turned out to be pretty routine, revealing no major health issues. However, Ella did promise herself that she wouldn't go four years without seeing her doctor again.

Get more sleep: For Ella, getting more sleep meant being disciplined about getting right to the tasks she needed to do when the girls went to bed. She couldn't do it every night, but she managed it about three out of four and felt more rested and energized as a result.

Build exercise into each day: Ella realized that dropping her gym membership didn't mean she had to stop working out. She bought a video of aerobic dance routines, and she and the girls started doing it together most evenings before dinner. As the days started getting longer, they also started going out for a run or to play tag after dinner. Ella told me, "We're having fun together, and I feel good that I'm modeling how important it is to move."

Month 2: Increasing Positivity

Count the Good Stuff—and keep a journal of it: This was harder to do than Ella thought it would be. She did want to do it—or at least she thought she did. But by the time she got ready to make her journal entries at night, she was tired and didn't feel like doing one more thing. Then she came up with a way to do it that also helped her relationship with her girls. They began their evening meal by telling each other about good stuff that had happened each day.

Do Random Acts of Kindness: At first, Ella thought this was silly, but she was willing to give it a try, especially at work. Sometimes she paid for her assistant's coffee order. She did a stack of copying herself instead of asking the secretary to do it. She helped organize the retirement party for a member of her team. This activity felt like an assignment at first, but Ella began to see results she hadn't expected. People at work started to be friendlier. Reflecting on this, she said, "I always thought of myself as a kind person, but I guess I got out of the habit of showing it." Doing random acts of kindness gave her character strengths a positive workout. She decided to expand by getting her girls in on it. They made a game of doing random helpful acts for neighbors and friends.

Do family maintenance: By the end of the second month, Ella was doing a much better job on family maintenance. Exercising with her kids, sharing the good stuff, and making a game of doing random acts of kindness together had brought them closer. To that she added signing up for a charity walk for breast cancer. It was yet another thing she could do with her girls, with the added benefit of connecting more to her community.

Month 3: Being More Mindful

Start meditating every day: Ella knew it would be helpful for her to learn to relax and refocus, but training herself to let go of thoughts instead of repeatedly going over and over and over lists of things she needed to do was a huge challenge. Evenings were out of the question. It worked better to find fifteen minutes each day to meditate at her desk. "I manage to escape my hamster wheel of over-thinking for maybe half of my meditation time now," she told me. "That's maybe seven whole minutes! But I'm going to keep at it."

Eat Mindfully: Ella realized that she and her girls had fallen into a bad habit of eating much too fast, so by the time the third month rolled around, she adjusted her plan to include eating mindfully. This was another area where she could model more positive behavior for her girls. The family also put a new rule in place to enhance their sense of connection during dinner: every few minutes, they'd all put their forks down and really talk.

Ella's Conclusions

Ella doesn't know if she'll keep making formal plans in the coming months. But her three-month experiment kick-started her into taking better care of herself. She feels better physically and says she's happier and more relaxed. Being more actively kind warmed up her office relationships. She's more thoughtfully exercising her character strength of fairness. Most importantly to her, she found that including her girls in her project had brought them closer. By doing more with and for others, she started feeling better about herself. Her enthusiasm is back. She's living with more genuine self-esteem.

Hal: Retired from Work, Not from Life

Hal is sixty-six years old and retired from an active job as a tree worker. When I asked him why he wanted to try out my approach to self-esteem, he had an unusual reason: "My kids and my wife tell me I'm turning into a grumpy old man. I think I'm fine, but they keep saying they're worried about me and that they aren't going to put up with my negativity."

"You really think things are fine?" I asked.

"Fine enough," he replied. "I don't believe in whining."

We talked about his values and where they had come from. He had very conservative parents and had gone straight to work after high school, then was drafted into the military and served a one-year tour of duty in Vietnam. He had come back to a world that, in his words, had gone nuts: "People protesting. Nuts! But what can you do?" he said. I learned that this was his default: a shrug and perseverance.

In the last two years, he'd retired from work that he loved and had lost several important friends who shared his values. Further, he was feeling at a distance from his family. The local pub was where he felt comfortable, so he stopped in most afternoons and had three or four beers before heading home to dinner. He knew he was drinking too much and agreed he was pretty pessimistic most of the time, but he felt he had reason to be. He wished he had more real friends but wondered if it was too late for that.

I could see that Hal was a good man. But as we talked about the meaning of genuine self-esteem, it was clear that he'd lost track of the doing part of the equation, mainly because he didn't know what to do. The visit to quadrant 1 (depressed self-esteem—a low sense of worthiness and low self-regard) that had followed his retirement had become a more permanent stay. So we developed a plan that focused on making stronger connections with his family, adding more positivity to his life, and finding other ways to relax besides drinking.

Hal's Plan

Character strengths: *responsibility, self-control, perseverance, intimacy, kindness*

Values: *It's important to do the right thing and be a good person, even when other people disagree about what the right thing is.*

Month 1 goal: *Find ways to connect more deeply and relax.*

Activities to work on that goal:

1. *Drink less*

2. *Volunteer*

Month 2 goal: *Keep connecting and increase positivity.*

Activities to work on that goal:

1. *Volunteer some more!*

2. *Deepen Your Friendships*

3. *Keep Things in Perspective*

Month 3 goal: *Deepen family relationships.*

Activities to work on that goal:

1. *Do Gratitude*

2. *Do Random Acts of Kindness*

What Happened

It didn't surprise me at all that Hal stuck with his program once he committed to it. After all, perseverance is one of his character strengths.

Month 1: Find Ways to Connect More Deeply and Relax

Drink less: Hal's visits to the pub were more about loneliness than drinking. He knew people there, and the bartender knew his name. He was willing to limit himself to one or two beers as a starting point. Since self-control is one of his strengths, that wasn't difficult. But he needed something to take the place of the social contact he got every time he walked into the pub. That's where volunteering came in.

Volunteer: Back in the day, Hal had coached his sons' Little League team, so I asked, "Why not get involved again?" The local organization was always in need of coaches, both to teach kids the game and to give some of the kids a much-needed male role model. With some reluctance (and grumpiness), he agreed to give it a try. In no time at all, he was umping third base two afternoons a week and Saturday mornings. He loved it! He still frequented the pub, but he also had practices and games to look forward to.

Month 2: Keep Connecting and Increase Positivity

Volunteer some more: Hal found out that one of the boys he was coaching was way behind in reading skills. He talked to the boy's mother and arranged to tutor him. Then he built on the boy's interest in baseball by using books and magazine articles about the sport. The boy thrived on the extra attention, but Hal will tell you he got more than he gave.

Deepen Your Friendships: Maintaining social contact can be a real problem as people get older. Friends start declining and dying. Age-mates who could become new friends may already have enough friends and not be looking for more. Hal definitely needed at least one or two new male friends to hang out with. The most obvious places to start were the Little League network and the pub. The other coaches and umpires are all about twenty years younger. Although they were fun to hang out with, Hal didn't see the potential for becoming real friends. However, he enjoyed talking with another regular at the bar who's also a veteran. Hal invited him to go to a baseball game. It's a start.

Keep Things in Perspective: As we worked together, Hal realized that he'd been grumpy because he'd been lonely and hadn't had a sense of purpose. Now that he was involved with his reading buddy and Little League, he was feeling reinvigorated. He was already starting to think about what he could contribute to the boys in his town when baseball season was over. He laughed when I told him Michael J. Fox's story of the lady giving birth in the tree, recognizing that he'd allowed himself to lose perspective. He often quoted it over the next few weeks as we continued to talk about how he wanted to live the next decade or so of his life.

Month 3: Deepen Family Relationships

Do Gratitude: Hal's lack of meaningful relationships with his grown sons was painful to him. He chose the activity "Do Gratitude" for the third month because he realized he had taken it for granted that his family knew he appreciated them. Verbalizing his gratitude was difficult at first, but it became easier as his sons and his wife responded by opening up to him more.

Do Random Acts of Kindness: As time went on, Hal came up with small things he could say or do for his sons and his wife that wouldn't stretch him too much. Doing little extras for them made him feel good about himself. He saw that his new demonstrations of love meant a lot to them.

Hal's Conclusions

Hal says that his three-month plan helped him reengage with life. Being a responsible guy, he hadn't felt okay being so stuck. He feels useful again. He exercised his character strengths of perseverance and kindness by volunteering, and especially by tutoring the boy with reading problems. To him, the most important outcome of his plan was that his relationships with his wife and sons began to improve. He feels good about that. Doing good and feeling good—that's what it means to have genuine self-esteem.

In Conclusion

When I read Gretchen Rubin's book *The Happiness Project*, I came on a passage that made me laugh out loud with recognition and appreciation. She said that by the time she had worked on her happiness project for a number of months, she realized that when she kept her resolutions and actually did the things that make her feel happier, she ended up feeling happier and acting more virtuously. "Do good, feel good; feel good, do good," she said (2009, 148). Like me, and now you, she had discovered the truth at the heart of genuine self-esteem. I couldn't say it better!

References

Adler, A. 1964. *Social Interest: A Challenge to Mankind.* Translated by J. Linton and R. Vaughan. New York: Capricorn Books.

Aronson, J. K. 2008. *Meyler's Side Effects of Psychiatric Drugs.* Amsterdam: Elsevier Science Books.

Bannink, F. 2012. *Practicing Positive CBT: From Reducing Distress to Building Success.* Chichester, West Sussex, UK: John Wiley and Sons.

Baumeister, R. F., J. D. Campbell, J. I. Krueger, and K. D. Vohs. 2003. "Does High Self-Esteem Cause Better Performance, Interpersonal Success, Happiness, or Healthier Lifestyles?" *Psychological Science in the Public Interest* 4(1): 1–44.

Benson, H. 1993. "The Relaxation Response." In *Mind Body Medicine: How to Use Your Mind for Better Health*, edited by D. Goleman and J. Gurin. New York: Consumer Reports Books.

Benson, H., and M. Klipper. 1975. *The Relaxation Response.* New York: William Morrow.

Block, G. 2004. "Foods Contributing to Energy Intake in the US: Data from NHANES III and NHANES 1999–2000." *Journal of Food Composition and Analysis* 17(3–4): 439–447.

Brach, T. 2013. *True Refuge: Finding Peace and Freedom in Your Own Awakened Heart.* New York: Bantam Books.

Branden, N. 2001. *The Psychology of Self-Esteem: A Revolutionary Approach to Self-Understanding That Launched a New Era in Modern Psychology.* San Francisco: Jossey-Bass.

Bronson, P., and A. Merryman. 2009. *Nurture Shock: New Thinking About Children.* New York: Twelve.

Cacioppo, J. T., and W. Patrick. 2009. *Loneliness: Human Nature and the Need for Connection.* New York: W. W. Norton.

Clinton, H. 2004. *Living History.* New York: Scribner.

Coan, J., H. Schaefer, and R. Davidson. 2006. "Lending a Hand: Social Regulation of the Neural Response to Threat." *Psychological Science* 17(12): 1032–1039.

Congreve, W. 1840. *Dramatic Works with Biographical and Critical Notices by Leigh Hunt.* London: Moxon.

Csikszentmihalyi, M. 1990. *Flow: The Psychology of Optimal Experience.* New York: Harper and Row.

Csikszentmihalyi, M. 1997. *Finding Flow: The Psychology of Engagement with Everyday Life.* New York: Basic Books.

Dalai Lama. 1998. *The Art of Happiness: A Handbook for Living.* New York: Riverhead Books.

Dreikurs, R. 1957. "The Courage to Be Imperfect" [speech, University of Oregon, July 25]. Available at http://www.carterandevans.com/portal/index.php/understanding-self-a-others /80-the-courage-to-be-imperfect. Accessed June 3, 2014.

Dreikurs, R. 1971. *Social Equality: The Challenge of Today.* Chicago: Henry Regnery Company.

Duckworth, A., C. Peterson, M. Matthews, and D. Kelly. 2007. "Grit: Perseverance and Passion for Long-Term Goals." *Journal of Personality and Social Psychology* 92(6): 1087–1101.

Dunbar, R. 2010. *How Many Friends Does One Person Need?* Cambridge, MA: Harvard University Press.

Edison, T. 1921. Interviewed in "Why Do So Many Men Never Amount to Anything?" *American Magazine* 91, January, 89.

Field, T., M. Diego, and M. Hernandez-Reif. 2001. "Preterm Infant Massage Therapy Research: A Review." *Infant Behavior and Development* 33(2): 115–124.

Fowler, J. H., and N. Christakis. 2008. "Dynamic Spread of Happiness in a Large Social Network: Longitudinal Analysis Over 20 Years in the Framingham Heart Study." *BMJ* 337: a2338.

Fox, M. J. 2013. Interviewed in "Back to His Future: Michael J. Fox Returns to TV." *Good Housekeeping*, October. Available at http://www.goodhousekeeping.com/family/celebrity-interviews/michael-j-fox. Accessed April 19, 2014.

Franks, D. D., and J. Marolla. 1976. "Efficacious Action and Social Approval as Interacting Dimensions of Self-Esteem: A Tentative Formulation Through Construct Validation." *Sociometry* 39(4): 324–341.

Fredrickson, B. 2009. *Positivity: Top-Notch Research Reveals the 3-to-1 Ratio That Will Change Your Life*. New York: Three Rivers Press.

Fry, R. 2013. "A Rising Share of Young Adults Live in Their Parents' Home." Pew Research Center report, August 1. Available at http://www.pewsocialtrends.org/files/2013/07/SDT-millennials-living-with-parents-07-2013.pdf. Accessed April 22, 2014.

Fulghum, R. 1988. *All I Really Need to Know I Learned in Kindergarten*. New York: Villard Books.

Graedon, J., and T. Graedon. 1995. *The People's Guide to Deadly Drug Interactions: How to Protect Yourself from Life-Threatening Drug-Drug, Drug-Food, Drug-Vitamin Combinations*. New York: St. Martin's Press.

Holt-Lunstad, J., T. B. Smith, and J. B. Layton. 2010. "Social Relationships and Mortality Risk: A Meta-analytic Review." *PLoS Medicine* 7(7): e1000316. doi:10.1371/journal.pmed.1000316.

Hubbard, E. 1923. *Selected Writings of Elbert Hubbard: His Mintage of Wisdom, Coined from a Life of Love, Laughter, and Work*. New York: William H. Wise.

Hyde, C. R. 1999. *Pay It Forward*. New York: Simon and Schuster.

Kabat-Zinn, J. 1993. "Mindfulness Meditation: Health Benefits of an Ancient Buddhist Practice." In *Mind Body Medicine: How to Use Your Mind for Better Health*, edited by D. Goleman and J. Gurin. New York: Consumer Reports Books.

Kabat-Zinn, J. 2005. *Wherever You Go, There You Are: Mindfulness Meditation in Everyday Life*. New York: Hyperion.

Kolbasovsky, A. 2008. *A Therapist's Guide to Understanding Common Medical Problems: Addressing a Client's Mental and Physical Health*. New York: W. W. Norton.

Kornfield, J. 2009. *The Wise Heart: A Guide to the Universal Teachings of Buddhist Psychology*. New York: Bantam.

Kornfield, J. 2011. *Bringing Home the Dharma: Awakening Right Where You Are*. Boston: Shambhala.

Lally, P., C. H. M. van Jaarsveld, H. W. W. Potts, and J. Wardle. 2010. "How Are Habits Formed: Modeling Habit Formation in the Real World." *European Journal of Social Psychology* 40(6): 998–1009.

Lecrubier, Y., G. Clerc, R. Didi, and M. Kieser. 2002. "Efficacy of St. John's Wort Extract WS 5570 in Major Depression: A Double-Blind, Placebo-Controlled Trial." *American Journal of Psychiatry* 159(8): 1361–1366.

Lyubomirsky, S. 2008. *The How of Happiness: A New Approach to Getting the Life You Want.* New York: Penguin Books.

Mandela, N. 2012. *Notes to the Future: Words of Wisdom.* New York: Simon and Schuster.

Maslow, A. 1954. *Motivation and Personality.* New York: Harper.

May, R., C. Rogers, and A. Maslow. 1984. *Politics and Innocence: A Humanistic Debate.* Dallas, TX: Saybrook.

Morrison, J. 1999. *When Psychological Problems Mask Medical Disorders: A Guide for Psychotherapists.* New York: Guilford Press.

Mruk, C. 2013. *Self-Esteem and Positive Psychology: Research, Theory, and Practice.* New York: Springer.

Neff, K. 2011. *Self-Compassion.* New York: William Morrow.

Niederhofer, H., and K. Pittschieler. 2006. "A Preliminary Investigation of ADHD Symptoms in Persons with Celiac Disease." *Journal of Attention Disorders* 10(2): 200–204.

O'Brien, E. J., and S. Epstein. 1983. *MSEI: The Multidimensional Self-Esteem Inventory.* Odessa, FL: Psychological Assessment Resources.

Peterson, C., and M. E. P. Seligman. 2004. *Character Strengths and Virtues: A Handbook and Classification.* New York: Oxford University Press.

Robbins, M. 2010. "The Law of Attraction: How to Act 'As If.'" *Huffpost Healthy Living*, March 25. Available at http://www.huffingtonpost.com/mike-robbins/the-law-of-attraction-how_b_513219.html. Accessed April 18, 2014.

Rogers, F. 2003. *The World According to Mister Rogers: Important Things to Remember.* New York: Hyperion.

Rubin, G. 2009. *The Happiness Project: Or, Why I Spent a Year Trying to Sing in the Morning, Clean My Closets, Fight Right, Read Aristotle, and Generally Have More Fun.* New York: Harper.

Schoenborn, C. A., and P. E. Adams. 2010. *Health Behaviors of Adults: United States, 2005–2007.* Washington, DC: National Center for Health Statistics. Vital Health Statistics series 10(245).

Seligman, M. E. P. 2002a. *Authentic Happiness: Using the New Positive Psychology to Realize Your Potential for Lasting Fulfillment*. New York: Free Press.

Seligman, M. E. P. 2002b. Interview in "Searching for a Happiness Strategy." *Los Angeles Times*, December 9. Available at http://articles.latimes.com/2002/dec/09/health/he-seligman9. Accessed April 19, 2014.

Seligman, M. E. P. 2007. *The Optimistic Child: A Proven Program to Safeguard Children Against Depression and Build Lifelong Resilience*. New York: Houghton Mifflin.

Seligman, M. E. P. 2011. *Flourish: A Visionary New Understanding of Happiness and Well-Being*. New York: Free Press.

Seligman, M. E. P., and S. F. Maier. 1967. "Failure to Escape Traumatic Shock." *Journal of Experimental Psychology* 74(1): 1–9.

Seligman, M. E. P., T. A. Steen, N. Park, and C. Peterson. 2005. "Positive Psychology Progress: Empirical Validation of Interventions." *American Psychologist* 60(5): 410–421.

Sheldon, K., and S. Lyubomirsky. 2007. "Is it Possible to Become Happier? (And If So, How?)." *Social and Personality Psychology Compass* 1(1): 129–145.

Stanley, E. H. 1894. *Speeches and Addresses of Edward Henry Fifteenth Earl of Derby, K.G. Vol. 1*. London: Longmans, Green, and Co.

Sutherland, S. 2012. "Bright Screens Could Delay Bedtime." *Scientific American Mind* 23(6). Available at http://www.scientificamerican.com/article/bright-screens-could-delay-bedtime. Accessed April 18, 2014.

Tafarodi, R. W., and W. B. Swann Jr. 1995. "Self-Liking and Self-Competence as Dimensions of Global Self-Esteem: Initial Validation of a Measure." *Journal of Personality Assessment* 65(2): 322–342.

Underwood, C. 2013. Interview in *The Making of the Sound of Music Live!* NBC, November 27.

Waldon, E. G. 2001. "The Effects of Group Music Therapy on Mood States and Cohesiveness in Adult Oncology Patients." *Journal of Music Therapy* 38(2): 212–238.

Wood, A. M., P. A. Linley, J. Maltby, T. B. Kashdan, and R. Hurling. 2011. "Using Personal and Psychological Strengths Leads to Increases in Well-Being over Time: A Longitudinal Study and the Development of the Strengths Use Questionnaire." *Personality and Individual Differences* 50(1): 15–19.

Marie Hartwell-Walker, EdD, is a licensed psychologist and marriage and family therapist in Massachusetts. She has a master's degree in counseling psychology from the Alfred Adler Institute of Chicago, and a master's and doctoral degree from the College of Education at the University of Massachusetts Amherst. She has authored numerous articles on psychology, parenting, and family life, is currently a feature writer and advice columnist for psychcentral.com and contributes to the divorce page of huffingtonpost.com.

Foreword writer **John M. Grohol, PsyD,** is founder, CEO, and editor in chief of psychcentral.com, the Internet's largest and oldest independent mental health social network. Since 1995, psychcentral.com has offered reliable, trusted information about mental health, psychology, social work, and psychiatry, and has hosted over 200 support groups for its readers. Grohol is coauthor of *Self-Help That Works*, author of *The Insider's Guide to Mental Health Resources Online*, and a published researcher.

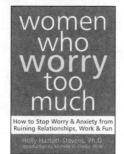

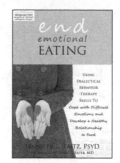
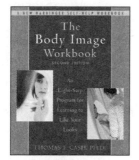

Register your **new harbinger** titles for additional benefits!

When you register your **new harbinger** title—purchased in any format, from any source—you get access to benefits like the following:

- Downloadable accessories like printable worksheets and extra content

- Instructional videos and audio files

- Information about updates, corrections, and new editions

Not every title has accessories, but we're adding new material all the time.

Access free accessories in 3 easy steps:

1. Sign in at NewHarbinger.com (or **register** to create an account).

2. Click on **register a book**. Search for your title and click the **register** button when it appears.

3. Click on the **book cover or title** to go to its details page. Click on **accessories** to view and access files.

That's all there is to it!

If you need help, visit:

NewHarbinger.com/accessories

new harbinger
CELEBRATING
40 YEARS